Target Vocabulary 2

Peter Watcyn-Jones

Illustrations by Neville Swaine

PENGUIN BOOKS

PENGUIN BOOKS

Published by the Penguin Group
Penguin Books Ltd, 27 Wrights Lane, London W8 5TZ, England
Penguin Putnam Inc., 375 Hudson Street, New York, New York 10014, USA
Penguin Books Australia Ltd, Ringwood, Victoria, Australia
Penguin Books Canada Ltd, 10 Alcorn Avenue, Toronto, Ontario, Canada M4V 3B2
Penguin Books (NZ) Ltd, 182–190 Wairau Road, Auckland 10, New Zealand

Penguin Books Ltd, Registered Offices: Harmondsworth, Middlesex, England

Published by Penguin Books 1994
10 9 8 7 6 5

Printed in England by Clays Ltd, St Ives plc
Set in 11/16 pt Linotron Century Schoolbook

Contents

Section Four: Education, books and the media 82

Section Five: Word-building ✗ 108

Section Six:
Adjectives, verbs and prepositions 127

Introduction

Target Vocabulary 2 follows on from *Target Vocabulary 1* and is intended for pre-intermediate/intermediate students and presents and practises approximately 1,500 key words. To facilitate learning, these have been arranged into areas of vocabulary. Altogether there are six main sections and each section has between 10 – 15 areas of vocabulary, closely linked to the main theme.

At the end of Section Three and Section Six there are mini tests called Check 1 and Check 2. These checks are for reinforcement and test the items in Sections 1–3 and 4–6 in a varied and interesting way.

Finally, to aid self-study, there is an answer key at the back of the book, plus a list of the key words used and the section(s) in which they appear.

In writing this book I have consulted a number of different dictionaries. The following can be warmly recommended:

Longman Dictionary of Contemporary English – new edition (Longman)
Collins Cobuild Essential English Dictionary (Collins)
Oxford Advanced Learners Dictionary (Oxford University Press)
The Penguin Wordmaster Dictionary, Manser and Turton (Penguin)
BBC English Dictionary (BBC English/HarperCollins)

Section One: People

Types of people 1

Write the missing words in the sentences below. Choose from the following:

acquaintance	employer	optimist	spectator
bachelor	fiancée	partner	spinster
boyfriend	lodger	pedestrian	tourist
colleague	motorist	pessimist	vegetarian
employee	neighbour	racist	widow

1 She is always expecting the best to happen. She is such an
_____.

2 A person who watches a sport or an event rather than takes part in it is called a _____.

3 Mrs Brown has been a _____ since her husband died seven years ago.

4 Pamela and Frank have been going out with each other since they met at university. He is the first _____ Pamela has ever wanted to marry.

5 Amanda and I own and run the company together. She is my
_____.

6 A _____ is someone who visits another country or district for a holiday.

7 'Is James married yet?'
'No, he's still a _____.'

8 A _____ is someone who goes everywhere on foot.

9 I work for IBM. They are my _____.

10 She never eats any sort of meat. She's a _____.

11 Julie and I work together. She is my _____.

12 Someone who drives a car is called a _____.

13 He is always expecting the worst to happen. He is such a
_____.

14 A woman who has never married is called a _____.

15 Pauline and Brian have just got engaged. Pauline is Brian's
_____.

16 If you work for yourself you are called self-employed. If you work
for someone else, you are called an _____.

17 He thinks British people are far superior to other nationalities
and looks down on most foreigners. He's a _____.

18 Mary lives next door to me. She's my _____.

19 Tom rents a room in our house. He's our _____.

20 I don't know her really well. She's just an _____.

Types of people 2

*Write the missing words in the sentences below. Choose from the
following:*

ancestor	gossip	orphan	successor
boss	heir	patient	survivor
celebrity	invalid	predecessor	tenant
client	landlord	refugee	twin
customer	opponent	rival	victim

1 I rent my flat from him. He is my _____.

2 He has been driven from his country for political reasons. He is
a _____.

3 Who had the job before you? Who was your _____?

4 Her appearance on a television quiz programme has made her
into a local _____. Most people recognize her when
they see her.

4

5 Mrs Brown comes into my shop at least once a day. She is a favourite _____ of mine.

6 Who is the person in charge here? Who is the _____?

7 His niece, Susan, will inherit everything when he dies. She is his only _____.

8 An _____ of hers, her great-grandfather, came from Norway.

9 The nurse told the next _____ to go in and see the doctor.

10 Peter Williams takes over after me. He is my _____.

11 My uncle is an accountant. Most of the people he deals with are actors and pop stars. Perhaps his most famous _____ is Mick Jagger.

12 Paula and Sally were born on the same day. Paula is Sally's _____ and most people find it very difficult to know who is who as they look so alike.

13 An _____ is someone who is disabled or very ill and needs to be cared for by someone else.

14 The only _____ in the recent plane crash near Paris was a nine-month-old baby. Everyone else on the plane died.

15 In the 1992 American Presidential election, George Bush's main _____ for the post of President was Governor Bill Clinton.

16 A teenager was killed in a fight outside a local disco on Saturday, but the police have not yet named the _____.

17 Who is playing against you in the tennis match? Who is your _____?

18 A _____ is someone who enjoys talking about other people's private lives.

19 She became an _____ at the age of seven when both her parents were killed in a car crash.

20 She didn't own her house, she was just a _____.

Describing people: Physical appearance

1 *The following words can be used to describe people. Write each word in the correct box. To help you there are some words already in the boxes.*

above average height
attractive
below average height
dark-haired
dark-skinned
fair-haired
going bald
good-looking
handsome
has a beard
has a moustache
in his/her early twenties
in his/her mid thirties
in his/her mid to late sixties
just turned fifty

muscular
of medium build
plump
pretty
quite old
quite tall
quite young
shoulder length
skinny
straight
swept back
tanned
thick, black
with a fringe
with a parting

Age
about (thirty)
elderly
old
young

Height

about (160) cm
of average height
short
tall

Figure/build

fat
has a good figure
slim
well-built

Hair

curly
grey
long, short
wavy

Other words

wears glasses
well-dressed
wearing (*describe clothes*)

2 *In the following dialogue, a police officer is questioning an eye-witness. After you have read it, look at the drawings and pick out the person you think the witness is describing.*

Police officer How old do you think he was?

Witness Well, he was quite young. In his late twenties, I'd say.

Police officer And was he tall?

Witness Yes, quite tall; taller than me, anyway. I'm 160 cm so he must have been about 175 to 180.

Police officer What about his build?

Witness Well, he was fairly slim. Not a bit muscular. Maybe even a bit skinny.

Police officer And what did he look like?

Witness Not very handsome. He had dark hair, but I can't really remember if it was long or short. But it was swept back. He didn't have a fringe or anything.

Police officer And did you notice what he was wearing?

Witness Oh yes! He was wearing jeans and this horrible striped sweater. Oh, and he had white trainers too.

Police officer Anything else?

Witness No, I don't think so. Oh, wait! He had an earring. In his left ear, I think.

Police officer Right, thank you. You've been very helpful.

3 *Now make up and act out your own dialogues, using the pictures on the opposite page. Whoever takes the part of the policeman must ask the questions and pick out the person he or she thinks the witness is describing. When you have done it once, change parts and do it again.*

Here are the questions the police officer asks:

- How old was (s)he?
- Was (s)he tall/short?
- What about his/her build?
- What did (s)he look like?
- What was (s)he wearing?
- Anything else you can remember?

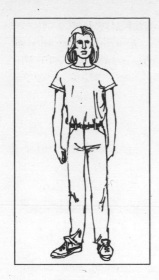  

Describing people: Character and personality 1

Here are twenty adjectives to describe a person's character or personality. Complete the sentences below with a suitable adjective from the list. Use each word once only.

affectionate	cheerful	forgetful	lively
bad-tempered	childish	friendly	materialistic
big-headed	clever	greedy	modest
bossy	cruel	honest	optimistic
brave	easy-going	impulsive	pessimistic

1 The Brown children were very _____ at school, so I'm not a bit surprised that they did so well at university.

2 Frank will never steal anything. You can trust him completely. He's so _____.

3 She won the race easily. But instead of boasting about it, she just said she was lucky. That's typical of her. She's so _____.

4 They're a very _____ couple. They're always showing their fondness and love for each other.

5 As a child he was very _____ and used to hit and kick animals — especially cats.

6 She always wants a bigger share than anyone else. She's so _____.

7 Gloria's always expecting the best to happen. She's such an _____ person.

8 Paul is always so angry and irritable. I've never met anyone quite as _____ as him.

9 My cousin is always happy and smiling. She's such a _____ person.

10 We had such a warm welcome when we were in Denmark. I had no idea that Danes were so _____.

12

11 Most people are far too _____ nowadays. All they seem interested in is buying more and more things, such as cars, TVs, and so on.

12 My grandfather always expects the worst to happen. He's really _____.

13 Don't keep telling Sharon how wonderful and talented she is. She'll get _____!

14 You'd better write his phone number down, Dave. You won't remember it otherwise. You know how _____ you are.

15 I could never be a childminder. Children are far too _____ for me. I'd be exhausted just watching them running around.

16 He loves telling people what to do. He's so _____.

17 Peter never worries very much or gets annoyed. He's a very _____ person.

18 My husband's very _____. If he sees something he just buys it without thinking about whether we can afford it or not.

19 Oh, grow up, Simon! Stop being so _____!

20 The police told her she was very _____ to jump into the river to rescue her sister.

Describing people: Character and personality 2

Here are another twenty adjectives to describe a person's character or personality. Again, complete the sentences below with a suitable adjective from the list. Use each word once only.

arrogant	kind	self-conscious	sympathetic
cautious	proud	selfish	talkative
cowardly	punctual	sensitive	vain
dishonest	reliable	strict	well-behaved
frank	self-confident	stubborn	witty

1 He is very sure he is going to succeed. He is extremely
_____.

2 Everyone thought it was _____ of him not to help his
friend when he was being attacked.

3 They say that women are generally more _____ than
men. They often find it easier to understand and be aware of
other people's problems.

4 It wasn't easy to have a conversation with George because he
wasn't very _____. Not a bit like his sister, Emily, who
never stopped talking.

5 Swedes and Germans have a reputation for being
_____. If you arrange a meeting with them they are
always on time.

6 He's so _____! He behaves as if he's so much better or
more important than the rest of us! I can't stand him!

7 Maureen's so _____. She's always coming out with
clever and amusing remarks. I wish I could make people laugh
the way she does.

8 Once his mind is made up, he won't listen to a word you say. He's
so _____.

9 You only care about yourself, don't you? You never think about
me or anyone else. You're so _____!

10 My neighbour is always so friendly and helpful. I don't think I've ever met such a _____ person as her.

11 Joanna spends hours looking at and admiring herself in the mirror. She's so _____.

12 He always wore a hat because he was very _____ about his bald patch.

13 It's a pleasure to look after my cousin's children. They're so _____. I wish my children had their good manners.

14 Mark is a very _____ person and never makes any decisions without looking into things very carefully first.

15 If Simon says he'll do it, then he will. You can trust him. He's very _____.

16 Although she was poor, she was very _____, and refused to accept any form of charity.

17 I wouldn't trust him with anything. He's so _____. He's always trying to cheat people.

18 Maureen was very _____ when I told her that my grandfather had died.

19 Years ago, teachers were very _____ and pupils weren't allowed to speak in class or ask a question without putting their hands up first.

20 I always try to be _____ with my friends. If they ask for my opinion, then I give it to them straight, even though they might not like it.

Follow up

Using the words from the above exercises, what qualities do you think are most important for the following people to have?

1 a teacher
2 a partner
3 a boss
4 a politician
5 a soldier

Describing people: Moods and feelings 1

Here are fifteen adjectives that describe moods and feelings. Each of the words fits in a gap in one of the sentences below. Supply the missing words. Use each adjective once only.

afraid	bored	embarrassed	nervous
angry	curious	excited	relieved
ashamed	depressed	guilty	sleepy
bitter	disappointed	lonely	

1 For the first six months after her husband died, she felt very
_____ and longed for company.

2 Many children, when they grow up and have their own families,
sometimes feel _____ at not seeing their parents very
often.

3 She was very _____ when her doctor told her that the
tests were negative. She didn't have cancer after all.

4 He always slept with the light on because he was _____
of the dark.

5 He felt very _____ and started to blush when his
mother started showing his girlfriend pictures of him as a baby.

6 Although he had been acting for over thirty years, he still felt
very _____ before every performance.

7 He became very _____ when I told him that someone
had damaged his car.

8 She was very _____ when she didn't get the job with
the BBC. She really thought she had got it.

9 I think I'd better go to bed. I'm feeling rather _____.

10 I'm _____ with watching TV all the time. Can't we go
out somewhere for a change?

11 The Prime Minister was still very _____ about the
way he had been forced to resign.

12 Bill's feeling really _____ at the moment. He's just lost his job and this morning his mother phoned him to say that his father was dying.

13 The children were very _____ at the thought of going to see the circus.

14 He felt _____ of himself for behaving so badly last night.

15 Why didn't Cathy and John get married? Do tell me. I'm very _____.

Describing people: Moods and feelings 2

Here are another fifteen adjectives to describe moods and feelings. Again, write the missing words in the sentences below. Use each adjective once only.

confused	frustrated	in a bad mood	shocked
disgusted	giddy	in a good mood	tense
envious	helpless	proud	upset
exhausted	hurt	restless	

1 I'm not angry. I'm just _____ that you didn't think you could trust me to look after your flat while you were away.

2 I can never stay in the same job or place for more than five or six years. I start to get _____ and want a change.

3 That's the last time I run a marathon! I'm absolutely _____!

4 Looking down from the top of high buildings always made him feel very _____.

5 He was very _____ about losing his wallet as, apart from money, it also contained his driving licence and credit cards.

6 She felt very _____ when she first moved to Paris. Everything was so different and she didn't speak the language very well.

7 'You're _____ today.'

'Yes, I know. Pete's just asked me to marry him.'

8 We were _____ when we saw how dirty the bathroom was and complained to the hotel manager.

9 You're looking very _____, Jane. Come on, try to relax.

10 They felt very _____ as their daughter stepped on to the stage to receive her prize.

11 Everyone in the village was deeply _____ to hear that the postman had been murdered.

12 He felt very _____ when his neighbour bought a new car.

13 'Sheila's _____. What's wrong?'

'Oh, her car was stolen last night, so she's had to come to work by bus today.'

14 She felt so _____ as she watched the child struggling in the river. There was nothing she could do. She couldn't swim.

15 I feel really _____. I've been trying to phone the theatre all morning but, every time I do, the line's engaged.

Follow up

Now choose a suitable adjective from the above two exercises to complete the following sentences. More than one answer may be possible for each sentence.

1 He was feeling _____ because it was his first day at his new school.

2 She had felt very _____ since her children had moved away from home.

3 They were feeling _____ as they waited for the pop star to appear on stage.

4 He felt _____ when he went to see his cousin's new house. It was really big, and it even had a swimming pool.

5 She felt very _____ when her mother volunteered to go on to the stage and try to tap dance.

6 They were _____ at his appearance. He looked terrible! It was hard to believe it was their son.

7 He felt _____ as he walked through the graveyard at midnight.

8 She felt _____ when her daughter phoned her to say she had arrived home safely. She had been really worried all evening.

9 He felt _____ when he didn't pass the exam. He thought he had done really well.

10 They were _____ because someone had broken into their car while they were shopping and stolen their car radio.

Jobs people do

1 *Look at the drawings below. How many jobs can you identify? Write your answers next to the numbers 1–18.*

1 _____	7 _____	13 _____
2 _____	8 _____	14 _____
3 _____	9 _____	15 _____
4 _____	10 _____	16 _____
5 _____	11 _____	17 _____
6 _____	12 _____	18 _____

2 *Now match the jobs (1–16) on the left with a suitable definition (a-p) from the right. Write your answers in the boxes on the next page.*

1 an accountant

2 a barrister

3 a caretaker

4 a childminder

5 a copywriter

6 a detective

7 a diver

8 a gardener

9 a head teacher

10 a lecturer

11 a psychiatrist

12 a receptionist

13 a scientist

14 a social worker

15 a stockbroker

16 an undertaker

a   looks after, takes care of gardens

b   is an expert in, for example, physics, chemistry or biology

c   looks after children during the day so that parents can go out to work

d   arranges funerals

e   is a lawyer who appears in court

f   is a doctor who treats people suffering from mental illness

g   buys and sells stocks and shares for people

h   helps companies with their bookkeeping and finances

i   is the person in charge of a school

j   helps and gives advice to people with serious financial or family problems

k   works under water using special breathing equipment

l   looks after a school, a block of flats, etc.

m   welcomes and deals with people arriving at a hotel

n   investigates crimes, trying to find the people who did them

o   teaches at a college or university

p   writes the words used in advertisements

1	2	3	4	5	6	7	8	9	10	11	12	13	14	15	16

Who's in charge?

The people (1–15) in the left-hand column are all in charge of the things (a–o) in the right-hand column. Match them correctly. Write your answers in the boxes at the bottom of the page.

1 a captain		a	the actors in a film or play
2 a chairperson		b	the nurses in a hospital
3 a chief		c	a tennis or cricket match
4 a conductor		d	a newspaper, a magazine
5 a curator		e	a ship, a football team
6 a director		f	a shop, a bank
7 an editor		g	a government
8 a governor		h	a meeting, a committee
9 a manager/manageress		i	a museum
10 a matron		j	a college
11 a president		k	an orchestra
12 a prime minister		l	an old people's home
13 a principal		m	a tribe
14 a warden		n	a republic
15 an umpire		o	a prison

1	2	3	4	5	6	7	8	9	10	11	12	13	14	15

Verbs to describe common bodily actions

Here are twenty verbs that describe some common bodily actions. Put them in the sentences below. Use each verb once only and make changes where necessary.

blink	crawl	lick	sneeze
blow one's nose	cry	lie down	touch
breathe	frown	nod	whistle
chew	kiss	smell	wink
cough	laugh	smile	yawn

1 Babies can't walk straight away. They usually _____ first.

2 The photographer asked everyone to _____ and look happy before he took the photo.

3 If you can't sing, you can always try to _____ the tune instead.

4 It is customary after a couple have just got married for the groom to _____ the bride.

5 Something in his eye made him _____ .

6 She _____ the stamp before sticking it onto the envelope.

7 You haven't stopped _____ for the past twenty minutes, Cheryl! You must be tired. You'd better go to bed.

8 The TV programme was really funny and they couldn't stop _____ .

9 You should always _____ your food properly before swallowing it.

10 There was a large sign in the museum telling people not to _____ anything.

11 The film was so sad that it made him _____ .

12 She bent down to _____ the flower.

13 I _____ at her to show that I was only joking.

14 Jane's father _____ as he read her terrible school report.

15 I'm feeling rather tired. I think I'll go and _____ for a while.

16 Stop sniffing, David! Take out your handkerchief and _____ properly!

17 She _____ her head to show that she agreed with me.

18 You wouldn't _____ so much if you gave up smoking!

19 I can't stop _____. I think I must have caught a cold.

20 The doctor asked her to _____ deeply.

Phrasal verbs

At the end of each section in this book you are going to learn some common and useful phrasal verbs. Try to learn these by heart as they will help you to read newspapers and magazines and to understand everyday conversations.

1 *Match up the phrasal verbs (1–10) with their meanings (a–j). Write your answers in the boxes at the bottom of the page.*

1 break down	a	match
2 carry on	b	leave the ground (e.g. an aeroplane)
3 clear up		
4 get on (with someone)	c	stop working (e.g. a machine)
5 go out		
6 go with	d	arrive
7 hang on	e	postpone
8 put off	f	stop raining or being cloudy and turn sunny
9 take off		
10 turn up	g	stop burning (e.g. a fire)
	h	continue
	i	wait
	j	have a good relationship with someone

1	2	3	4	5	6	7	8	9	10

2 *Now complete the following dialogues with a suitable phrasal verb. Choose from the list on page 27 and make any necessary changes.*

1 A: What do you think of the curtains?

  B: They don't really _____ the carpet, do they? You need something darker.

2 A: Was Mandy at the party on Saturday?

  B: No, she didn't _____.

3 A: You're late!

  B: I'm sorry, but my car _____.

4 A: Are you going to the meeting tonight?

  B: Haven't you heard? It's been _____ until next week.

5 A: Oh no! It's started raining!

  B: Don't worry, it'll _____ soon.

6 A: Which gate number for flight SK 505 to Copenhagen, please?

  B: Gate 25. But you'd better hurry, it _____ in fifteen minutes.

7 A: Put some more wood on the fire, please, Alan.

  B: Too late! It's _____!

8 A: Shall we stop for a break now?

  B: No, let's _____ for a while longer.

9 A: Aren't you friends with Mark any more?

  B: No, we just don't _____ these days.

10 A: Is Mr Reed at work today?

  B: _____. I'll just check.

Section Two:
Towns, travel and transport

In the town

1 *Look at the drawings on the next two pages and then write the numbers 1–25 next to the following words.*

advertisement	multi-storey	pillar box
bridge	car park	public
building site	newspaper	conveniences
bus stop	vendor	road sign
café	park	subway
department	parking meter	taxi rank
store	pavement	telephone box
kerb	pedestrian	tower block
lamp-post	crossing	traffic island
litter bin	pedestrian	traffic lights
	precinct	

2 *Now choose words from the above list to complete the following sentences.*

1 The new _____ for the latest breakfast cereal could be seen all over the town.

2 The car had to stop because the _____ were red.

3 Have you got any coins for the _____? Enough to stay here for an hour, anyway.

4 Don't throw your rubbish on the floor! Use the _____.

5 Harrods is a very famous _____ in London.

6 The safest way to cross a busy road is to use the _____.

7 Is there a _____ around here somewhere? I need to post this letter.

8 If you need to go to the toilet, the _____ are outside the market.

9 He got stuck on the _____ half-way across the road.

10 In some towns, pedestrians can use a _____ to go under a busy road.

Travelling by road

1 *Look at the drawings on the next page and then write the numbers 1–20 next to the following words.*

bypass	diversion	junction	outside lane
central reservation	flyover	lay-by	roundabout
crash barrier	grass verge	level crossing	service area
crossroads	hard shoulder	middle lane	slip road
cycle path	inside lane	motorway	underpass

2 *Now choose words from the previous exercise to complete the following definitions.*

1 You enter or leave a motorway by a _____.

2 A _____ is a space next to a main road where you can park your car out of the way of the other traffic.

3 A _____ is a road that takes traffic round the edge of a town rather than through its centre.

4 A _____ is a special route arranged for traffic when the normal route cannot be used.

5 The _____ is the narrow piece of ground at the side of a road which is usually covered with grass.

6 People driving fast cars on motorways try to stay in the _____ as much as possible.

7 An _____ is a road which goes underneath another road or a railway line.

8 A _____ is a place where a road and a railway line cross each other. It is usually protected by gates or a barrier that shuts off the road while a train passes.

9 A _____ is a place where roads join.

10 The _____ is the area at the side of a motorway where you are allowed to stop if your car has broken down.

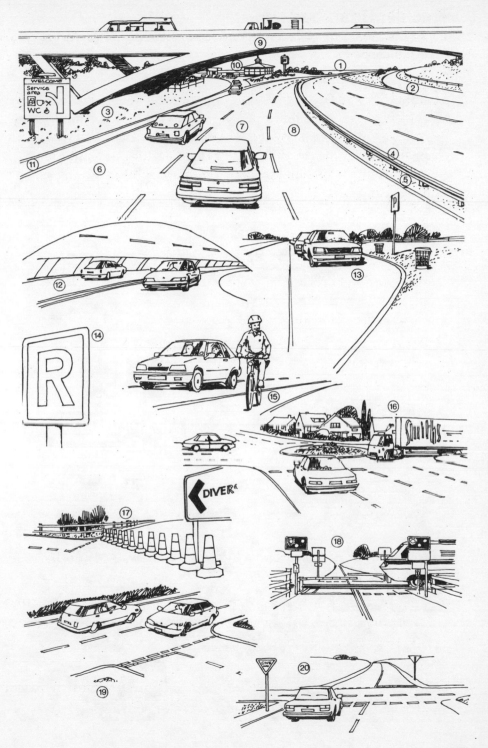

Vehicles: Road transport

Look at the drawings below and write the numbers 1–16 next to the following words.

ambulance	fire engine	motorbike	scooter
bicycle	hatchback	pick-up truck	sports car
bus	juggernaut	police car	taxi
coach	lorry	saloon car	van

Vehicles: Other forms of transport

Look at the drawings below and write the numbers 1–16 next to the following words.

barge	horse and cart	liner	speedboat
canoe	hot-air balloon	motor boat	train
car ferry	hovercraft	plane	tram
dinghy	lifeboat	rowing boat	yacht

Parts of a car
Exterior

*Look at the drawing below and write the numbers 1–20 next to the
following words.*

aerial	indicator	tyre
bonnet	lock	wheel
boot	number plate	windscreen
bumper	petrol cap	windscreen
door handle	rear light	wiper
exhaust pipe	rear window	wing
headlight	roof rack	wing mirror

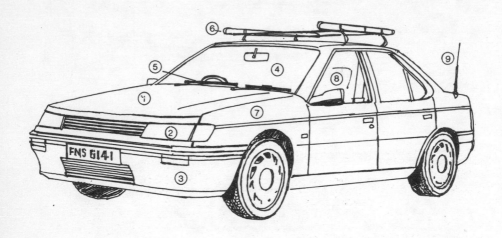

Interior

Look at the drawing below and write the numbers 1–20 next to the following words.

accelerator	gear lever	passenger seat
brake pedal,	glove	petrol gauge
foot brake	compartment	rear-view
car radio	handbrake	mirror
choke	heater	seat-belt
clutch	horn	speedometer
dashboard	ignition	steering wheel
driver's seat	indicator switch	

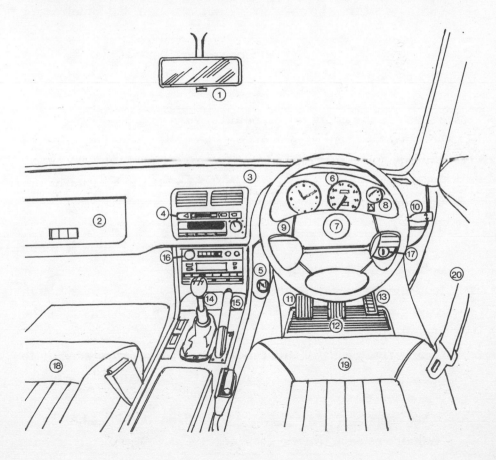

Verbs to do with driving

Write the missing words in the sentences below. Choose from the following list and make any changes that may be necessary.

accelerate	dip one's headlights	park
brake	do a U-turn	reverse
break down	give way	skid
break the speed limit	keep to the speed limit	stall
change gear	overtake	tow

1 He usually _____ when he's driving. So if the sign says 90, then he never drives at more than 90 kilometres per hour.

2 To _____ means to drive backwards.

3 You usually _____ to make a car slow down or stop.

4 When driving at night you should always _____ when you see a car coming towards you. Otherwise you can blind the driver.

5 This car can _____ from 0–100 kilometres per hour in under ten seconds.

6 To _____ a car means to drive past it.

7 If a car _____ another one, it pulls it along behind it, usually using a rope or a chain.

8 It is always very difficult to _____ in the High Street, so we usually go to one of the large car parks near the station.

9 One of the most difficult things when learning to drive is to _____ smoothly. That's why many people prefer automatic cars.

10 When a car _____, it turns round in a half circle then drives back the way it came.

11 He was fined for _____. He was doing over 100
   kilometres per hour in a built-up area where the limit was 50.
12 In Britain, when you reach a roundabout you should always
   _____ to traffic on your right.
13 When a car _____, the engine stops suddenly,
   because there is not enough power or speed to keep it going. This
   can sometimes happen when you first drive a car on a cold, frosty
   morning.
14 He was late for the meeting because his car _____
   just outside Brighton.
15 It is very easy for a car to _____ and go out of
   control if the roads are wet or icy.

Road signs
*Look at the drawings of the road signs on the next page and write
down what they mean. Choose from the following list. (You will not
use all the phrases in the list.)*

Airport	No left turn	Road narrows
Bend to right	No overtaking	Road works
End of motorway	No parking	School crossing
Give way	No right turn	patrol
Level crossing	No stopping	Start of
ahead	No through road	motorway
Maximum speed	No U-turns	Uneven road
No entry	One way street	

1 _____

2 _____

3 _____

4 _____

5 _____

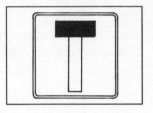

6 _____

7 _____

8 _____

9 _____

10 _____

11 _____

12 _____

13 _____

14 _____

15 _____

Travelling by train

Read the passage below and supply the missing words. Choose from the following list. One of the words will be used more than once.

buffet car	left-luggage	through train
carriage	office	ticket collector
catch	luggage rack	ticket office
change	no smoking	tickets
compartments	platform	timetable
departures board	railway station	train
inter-city	restaurant car	trolley
express	return	window seat

David Perry went to the (1)_____ to pick up a suitcase he had left there earlier in the day. Then he went to the (2)_____ and asked for a second-class (3)_____ to Hastings.

Five minutes later he was checking his London–Hastings (4)_____ to see what time his (5)_____ left. There was one at 12.15 from (6)_____ 12. He checked his watch. It was 11.55.

'Good,' he thought. 'I can (7)_____ that one.'

As he walked towards (8)_____ 12, an old lady stopped him. She was pushing a (9)_____ which contained two large suitcases. She asked him if there was a train to Southampton soon. He looked up at the large (10)_____ above their heads. He soon found what he was looking for.

'Yes, there's a train leaving in fifteen minutes from (11)_____ 6,' he said to her. 'It's an (12)_____.'
The old lady thanked him, and David hurried along.

The (13)_____ were quite full by the time he reached the (14)_____. He got into the second (15)_____ and, after putting his suitcase on a (16)_____, managed to find a (17)_____. It was a (18)_____ compartment. David was pleased as he was allergic to cigarette smoke.

Ten minutes after the train had left the (19)_____, the (20)_____ came round to check people's (21)_____.

'Is this a (22)_____?' David asked.

'No, you'll have to (23)_____ at Eastbourne.'

'And can you get something to drink on the train?'

'Sorry, sir, there's no (24)_____ or (25)_____ on this service, I'm afraid.'

'Ah well, never mind,' David thought to himself. 'We'll soon be in Hastings.'

Travelling by plane

Read the passage below and supply the missing words. Choose from the following list. One of the words will be used more than once.

airline ticket	Customs	landed
airport	departure lounge	long-term
aisle	departures board	car park
baggage reclaim	duty free	non smoking
boarding	flight	passport
boarding pass	Gate	passport control
check in (v)	hand luggage	security check
check-in desk	immigration	Terminal
conveyor belt	officer	took off

After Penny Dawson had parked her car in the (1)_____ at (2)_____ 3 at Heathrow (3)_____, she made her way to the British Airways (4)_____. She was going to Paris for the weekend and only had one small suitcase to (5)_____. She also had a shoulder-bag, but that would go as (6)_____.

She handed over her (7)_____ to the girl and asked if she could sit in a (8)_____ seat.

'(9)_____ or window?'

'(10)_____, please,' Penny answered.

The British Airways girl gave her a (11)_____ and wished her a pleasant (12)_____. Jenny thanked her and made her way towards the (13)_____. Before she got there she had to go through a (14)_____ where her bag was X-rayed, and then she had to show her (15)_____ to an (16)_____.

The first thing she did was to buy some cheap (17)_____
goods for the friends she was going to stay with. Then she sat down
near the large (18)_____ to wait for her flight to be called.

Eventually, the board showed that Flight BA 325 to Paris was now
(19)_____ through (20)_____ 25.

The plane (21)_____ on time and, forty-five minutes
later, (22)_____ at Charles de Gaulle airport in Paris.
Once off the plane, she followed her fellow-passengers to the
(23)_____ area to pick up her suitcase. Before getting
there she had to go through (24)_____ and show her
passport again.

After a short wait, her suitcase finally appeared on the
(25)_____. She picked it up and quickly passed through
(26)_____ where her friends, she hoped, would be waiting
for her.

Phrasal verbs

1 *Match the phrasal verbs (1–10) with their meanings (a–j). Write your answers in the boxes at the bottom of the page.*

1 call for	a	return (a thing) to its owner
2 call off	b	begin a journey
3 fill in	c	connect (by telephone)
4 get in	d	complete (a form, etc.)
5 give back	e	collect someone
6 look up	f	tolerate
7 put through	g	reduce the noise (of a radio, television, etc.)
8 put up with		
9 set off	h	search for something (in a dictionary, encyclopedia, etc.)
10 turn down	i	cancel, abandon
	j	arrive home

1	2	3	4	5	6	7	8	9	10

2 *Now complete the following dialogues with a suitable phrasal verb. Choose from the above list and make any necessary changes.*

1 A: What does the word 'inevitable' mean?

   B: I've no idea. _____ it _____ in a dictionary.

2 A: I'd like to join the tennis club, please.

   B: Certainly. Just _____ this application form.

3 A: Are you leaving early tomorrow morning?

   B: No, not really. We think we'll _____ at about 10.30.

4 A: What was the rock concert like?

   B: Didn't you hear? They had to _____ it _____
   because the lead singer was ill.

5 A: Pam's husband never helps in the home. He doesn't even do
   the washing-up.

   B: It's a disgrace! I don't know how she _____ it!

6 A: Here's the book you asked to borrow.

   B: Thanks. I'll _____ it _____ to you tomorrow.

7 A: What time shall we go to Bob's party?

   B: Why don't I _____ you at about 7.30?

8 A: That music's very loud!

   B: Shall I _____ it _____?

9 A: You didn't phone me last night!

   B: I know. I'm very sorry but I didn't _____ until midnight.

10 A: Could I speak to Mr Barker, please?

   B: One minute, caller, I'll just _____ you _____.

Section Three:
Holidays and entertainment

Places to stay on holiday

Write the missing words in the sentences below. Choose from the following:

bed and breakfast	chalet	motel
boarding house	guest house	self-catering
campsite	holiday camp	spa
caravan	hotel	youth hostel

1 If you have a tent, you can always stay at a _____.

2 A _____ is a place with a spring of mineral water, where people go for their health — usually to try to cure various diseases.

3 In Britain you can stay the night at a _____ place. This is usually a private home and is fairly cheap. It is sometimes called a _____.

4 The Ritz is a famous _____ in London. So is the Dorchester.

5 A _____ is a large private home where you can pay to stay and have meals. These are very common at seaside resorts.

6 Many people take a _____ with them on holiday. In many ways, it is like taking your home with you. And the big advantage, of course, is that you can stop and sleep almost anywhere.

7 A _____ is a place where large numbers of people, especially families, stay. Here, all the food, accommodation and entertainment is included in the price. You usually stay in a wooden building called a _____.

8 A_____ is specially built for motorists, with a space to park your car next to the rooms.

9 Many young people and those on walking or cycling holidays stay at a _____. This is usually very basic and cheap, and you often have to sleep in the same room as others.

10 Many people when they go abroad stay at a _____ cottage or flat. Here, they have to do all the cooking themselves.

Booking a holiday

In the following extract from a dialogue at a travel agency the lines are mixed up. Put them in the correct order. Some numbers have already been filled in.

___ – Amsterdam.

___ – Did you say June 5th?

___ – Right. Now if I could just have some details from you...

1 – Good morning. Can I help you?

___ – Two weeks, if possible.

___ – June 3rd. Yes, we have room. How many of you will there be?

3 – In which month?

___ – No, the 3rd. It's July 5th.

___ – Yes, I'd like to book a coach holiday, please. To Holland.

___ – I see. Well, the one on June 3rd sounds all right. I'll take that.

___ – And where exactly in Holland?

___ – Two weeks? Right. We have trips to Amsterdam on June 3rd, June 18th, July 5th and July 20th.

___ – Just me.

___ – Amsterdam. I see. And for how long?

___ – June or July.

Things you can do on holiday

Match the verbs (1–14) on the left with a suitable word or words (a-n) on the right. Write your answers in the boxes at the bottom of the page.

1	buy	a	a really good time
2	eat	b	postcards home
3	get	c	on the beach
4	go	d	museums and art galleries
5	go on	e	a suntan
6	have	f	speaking a foreign language
7	hire	g	in the pool
8	lie	h	some souvenirs
9	meet	i	a car
10	practise	j	sightseeing
11	send	k	lots of photographs
12	swim	l	at local restaurants
13	take	m	new people
14	visit	n	an excursion

1	2	3	4	5	6	7	8	9	10	11	12	13	14

Extracts from holiday brochures

Write the missing words in the extracts below. Choose from the following list. Use each word once only.

Asia	explore	scuba diving
bays	holiday-makers	sightseeing
beaches	markets	spectacular
breathtaking	Mediterranean	sunshine
capital	mountains	trip
coast	palm	unspoilt
cuisine	picturesque	villages
destinations	restaurants	
dishes	scenery	

The island of Majorca is still one of most popular holiday (1)_____ in the (2)_____. It offers a range of (3)_____ from the chain of (4)_____ which run across the west coast to the beautiful sandy (5)_____ with a backdrop of spectacular cliffs.

Visit the (6)_____, Palma, with majestic Bellver Castle and an abundance of shops. In the (7)_____, you'll see a combination of ancient and modern on a smaller scale with plenty of opportunities for watersports or sunbathing. There are numerous, excellent (8)_____ serving a wide variety of Spanish cuisine and traditional local (9)_____. Majorca is also famous for its festivals, nightlife and Mallorquin dancing.

Lanzarote, lying only 100 kilometres off the (10)_____ of Africa, boasts an excellent (11)_____ record and a (12)_____ volcanic landscape and huge, equally dramatic stretches of fine sandy beaches.

(13)_____ the green shuttered, white-washed villages that nestle amongst looming lunar rock formations and waving (14)_____ trees, and don't miss a (15)_____ to Fire Mountain, the island's live volcano.

Fortunately for the many (16)_____ that visit the island, Lanzarote has much more to offer than just natural beauty. Watersport enthusiasts can enjoy windsurfing and (17)_____. You can purchase many duty free goods in the shops and sample the local (18)_____ at one of the island's many restaurants. A hire car is an easy way to explore Lanzarote's (19)_____, sleepy villages.

Stretching from Europe to (20)_____ and the Middle East, Turkey, with its mixture of Eastern and European influences, is one of the most exotic and (21)_____ places you can visit.

The scenery is (22)_____ with mountains sweeping down to silver beaches, and hundreds of little (23)_____ are dotted along the coast.

Turkey's (24)_____ are a bargain hunter's dream with their cheap leather goods, brass items and of course Turkish carpets. The local food is marvellous and cheap, with numerous restaurants for you to sample. (25)_____ enthusiasts won't be disappointed either – historical monuments stand as superb reminders of a bygone age, with Ephesus one of the country's ancient treasures.

Other useful holiday words

Write the missing words in the sentences below. Choose from the following:

balcony	foreign currency	phrase-book
beauty spot	guidebook	resort
brochures	holiday-makers	sunbathing
cruise	itinerary	view
excursion	package tour	visa

1 A _____ is a holiday which includes travel, hotels, meals, etc. It is usually planned and people travel in fairly large groups.

2 I like to come back from my holidays with a good suntan, so I usually spend most of the day _____ on the beach.

3 Before deciding where to go on holiday, we always read lots of different _____ which we get from our local travel agency.

4 I'm just going to the bank to get some _____ for my trip to France next week.

5 In the winter, her parents always spent two weeks at a ski _____ in Austria.

6 When they booked in at the hotel, they asked for a room with a _____ of the beach and a _____ they could sit out on in the evenings.

7 If you don't speak the language in the country you're visiting, it's a good idea to take a _____ with you.

8 In the summer, Brighton, Hastings and Eastbourne are always full of _____ — both British and foreign.

9 When she visited Florida, she stayed in Orlando and went on an _____ to the Kennedy Space Centre.

10 You still need to apply for a _____ to visit certain foreign countries.

11 A _____ is a place known for the beauty of its scenery.

12 An _____ is a plan of a journey, which includes the route, places to visit, and so on.

13 Before we visit a new place, we usually buy a _____ to get to know something about the place and to be able to plan our trip better.

14 I'd love to go on a world _____. Unfortunately, I don't think I ever will because I get seasick very easily.

At the seaside

Look at the drawing opposite and write the numbers 1–20 next to the following words.

beach	deck-chair	lifeguard	sea
beach hut	harbour	lighthouse	sea wall
beach-ball	horizon	pier	spade
bucket	hotel	sand	swimmer
cliff	kite	sandcastle	wave

Countries, nationalities and languages

Complete the following lists. Don't forget that in some countries they speak more than one language!

He or she comes from...	He or she is...	He or she speaks...
Australia	_____	_____
Austria	_____	_____
Belgium	_____	_____
Brazil	_____	_____
Britain	_____	_____
Canada	_____	_____
China	_____	_____
Denmark	_____	_____
Finland	_____	_____
France	_____	_____
Germany	_____	_____
Greece	_____	_____
Hungary	_____	_____
Italy	_____	_____
Japan	_____	_____
Norway	_____	_____
Poland	_____	_____
Portugal	_____	_____
Russia	_____	_____
Spain	_____	_____
Switzerland	_____	_____
Turkey	_____	_____

Public holidays and special occasions

On the left is a list of British public holidays and special occasions (1-8). Match them with a date or definition (a–h) on the right. Write your answers in the boxes at the bottom of the page.

1 bank holiday

2 birthday

3 Boxing Day

4 Christmas Day

5 Easter

6 New Year's Day

7 New Year's Eve

8 wedding anniversary

a January 1st

b December 26th

c a religious festival, usually during April

d December 31st

e an official non-religious public holiday

f the day every year when a couple remember and celebrate the day they got married

g December 25th

h the day every year when a person remembers and celebrates the day he or she was born

1	2	3	4	5	6	7	8

The world of music: Musical instruments

Look at the drawings of the musical instruments below and then write the numbers 1–25 next to the following words.

accordion	cymbal	kettledrum	triangle
bagpipes	double bass	oboe	trombone
banjo	flute	organ	trumpet
bassoon	French horn	piano	tuba
bongoes	harmonica	saxophone	viola
cello	harp	tambourine	violin
clarinet			

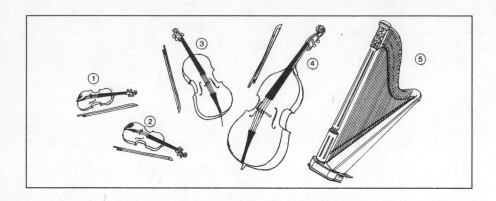

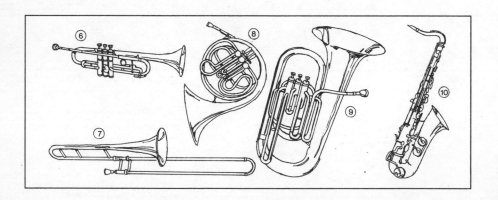

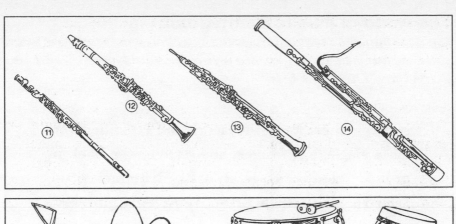

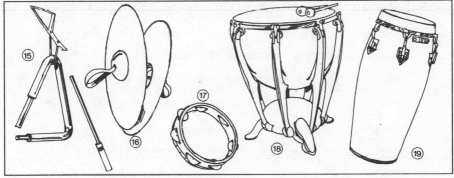

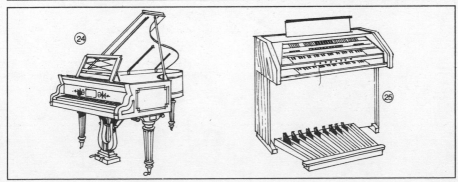

The world of music: A pop group

*Read the following text and study the drawing on the next page. When you have finished, write the word printed in **bold** type in the text next to the correct numbers 1–16.*

A pop group can have many forms, but a traditional one has a single **lead singer**, and sometimes a **backing group**. There is nearly always a **drummer** sitting behind his or her **drum kit** and two or three **guitarists** playing electric guitars. The person playing **lead guitar** is usually a very good guitarist and has all the solos. The person playing **bass guitar**, which is the biggest of the electric guitars, provides a strong, often pounding bass rhythm. Sometimes, especially for a slower, quieter ballad, one of them might play an **acoustic guitar**. The difference is that electric guitars always have to be plugged into an **amplifier**. The singer sings into a **microphone** and behind him or her are usually several enormous **loudspeakers**. Nowadays there is nearly always a **keyboard player**. He or she plays a range of **synthesizers** and possibly an **electric piano**. Finally, some groups have a **saxophone player** and might even have one or two **dancers**.

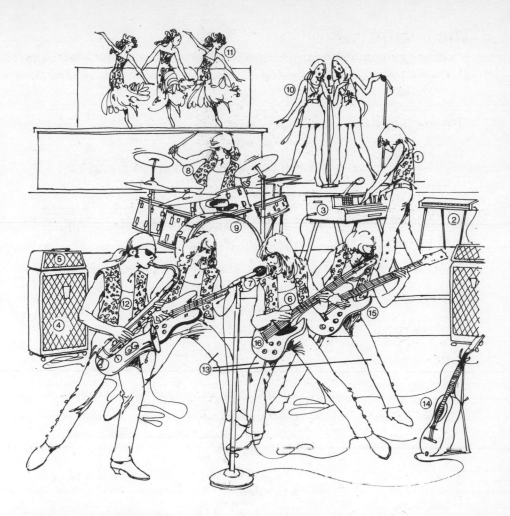

Write the words here.

1 _____

2 _____

3 _____

4 _____

5 _____

6 _____

7 _____

8 _____

9 _____

10 _____

11 _____

12 _____

13 _____

14 _____

15 _____

16 _____

The theatre

1 *Who's who in the theatre? Match the words (1–14) on the left with a suitable definition (a–n) on the right. Write your answers in the boxes at the bottom of the page.*

1 actor, actress

2 audience

3 cast

4 company

5 choreographer

6 critic

7 director

8 playwright

9 prompter

10 set designer

11 stage hand

12 stage manager

13 understudy

14 usher, usherette

a the person who writes reviews of new plays, musicals, etc.

b all the people who act in a play or a musical

c learns another actor's part in order to be able to take his place if he or she is ill or unable to perform

d reminds the actors of their next line in a speech if they forget it

e shows people coming to watch the play or musical to their seats

f makes up or arranges the steps for the dancers who perform on stage

g designs the scenery, etc. on stage

h a group of actors, singers or dancers who work together, e.g. The Royal Shakespeare _____

i the people who come to watch a play or a musical

j helps behind the scenes during a production, e.g. by moving scenery, etc.

k a person who writes plays

l is responsible for everything that happens on stage during a performance

m a person whose job is acting

n decides how a play is performed; tells the actors what to do

1	2	3	4	5	6	7	8	9	10	11	12	13	14

2 *Write the missing words in the sentences below. Choose from the following:*

aisle	curtain	interval	rehearse (verb)
applause	dress	matinée	row
auditorium	rehearsal	(orchestra) pit	stage
box office	dressing-room	performance	stalls
circle	first night	programme	wings
(or balcony)	foyer		

1 We picked up the tickets we had ordered at the theatre
 _____ .

2 The _____ is the large area just inside the main doors
 of a theatre where people meet and wait, while the
 _____ is the part of a theatre where the audience sit.

3 He was given the Evening Standard Actor of the Year award for
 his _____ in *Cyrano de Bergerac*.

4 We walked down the _____ behind an usher as he
 showed us to our seats in _____ F.

5 The _____ was terrible. Several of the actors forgot
 their lines, one or two dancers fell over and there was a problem
 with the lighting. Let's hope the play's a lot better when it opens
 on Saturday.

6 When you buy tickets you can choose to sit downstairs in the
 _____ or upstairs in the _____.

7 If you can't get to see the play in the evening, you can always go
 to the _____ or afternoon performance.

8 The audience really loved the new musical, as they showed by
 their loud _____ at the end.

9 The _____ is the area where the actors stand and
 perform.

10 I never go to see a play on its _____. I prefer to wait a
 few weeks. It's usually better then.

11 In front of the stage is an area where the musicians sit. This is called the _____.

12 If you want to know more about the play or the actors in it, you can always buy a _____ before the performance.

13 The audience became silent as the _____ went up and the play began.

14 Before going on stage, the actors often wait in the _____, that is, the area to the side of the stage, hidden from the audience.

15 There is usually a short _____ of about 15–20 minutes between the acts of a play.

16 They normally _____ for at least two months before they perform in public.

17 The actors put on their costumes and make-up in the _____.

The cinema

1 *Read the definitions below, then write the numbers 1–15 next to the following types of film.*

action/adventure film	fantasy film	musical
cartoon	foreign film	science fiction film
comedy	horror film	thriller
drama	juvenile film	war film
disaster movie	love story	western

1 Film dealing with major disasters, such as earthquakes, large fires, plane crashes, etc.

2 In this film, love and romance are the key elements.

3 Film to do with some aspect of war.

4 Any non English-speaking film.

5 In this film, excitement is generated from action sequences.

6 Film aimed at children and young people.

7 Film which sets out to make the audience laugh.

8 Film about the American wild west, usually with cowboys, indians and gunfights.

9 Film set in the future, and often to do with space travel, robots, etc.

10 Film where the characters and/or situations could not exist in real life. Often deals with magic and mystery, fantastic voyages, etc.

11 A very dramatic film where tension and suspense is deliberately maintained and is a central feature of the plot.

12 In this film, the focus is on human relationships rather than action.

13 A film where the main aim is to terrify the audience.

14 Also called an animated film. Here the film is made by photographing drawings rather than using live actors.

15 A film where the emphasis is on music. It usually contains lots of songs.

2 *Read the film reviews below, then decide what type of film each one is. Choose from the types of film above and write your answers under each title.*

Danny, the Champion of the World (1989)

1 *Type:* _____

Set in the 1950s, this tells the story of Danny, a 9-year-old living with his father. When their peaceful life in a caravan is threatened by a local developer who has bought all the surrounding land except their tiny plot, the boy finds a way to teach him a lesson. A nicely made and fun film for kids.

The Time Guardian (1987)

2 *Type:* _____

Imaginative tale about a group of time-travellers from the future who arrive in a small Australian town to tell inhabitants that unstoppable killer cyborgs from the 40th century are on their way.

Platoon (1986)

3 *Type:* _____

A realistic look at the experiences of a front-line American soldier in Vietnam that says what has been said many times before: war is hell and meaningless.

Earthquake (1974)

4 *Type:* _____

An epic tale with a star-studded cast about the destruction of Los Angeles, as the most catastrophic earthquake of all time rips through Southern California, affecting the lives of all who live there. Excellent special effects make up for the tedious and clichéd plot.

Raiders of the Lost Ark (1981)

5 *Type:* _____

Steven Spielberg's all-action blockbuster with Harrison Ford as Indiana Jones, who is sent to find the legendary biblical Ark of the Covenant before it can be stolen and used by the Nazis in their plan for world domination. A spectacular multi-million dollar version of the 1930s Saturday morning serials, and it works so well because of everybody's enthusiasm and sense of fun.

Hour of the Gun (1967)

6 *Type:* _____

Intriguing film starring James Garner as Wyatt Earp, the lawman who took on the Clanton gang at the OK Corral. Following the infamous gunfight, which left only half of the bandits dead, Earp rides off to bring the remaining members to justice.

Long Live the Lady! (1987)

7 *Type:* _____

It an director Ermanno Olmi's charming film about a gala dinner for a powerful old lady as seen through the eyes of a 16-year-old boy who is employed as a waiter for the evening. Warmly observed and amusing. English sub-titles.

Lady in a Cage (1964)

8 *Type:* _____

A tense tale of suspense starring Olivia de Havilland as a wealthy widow who finds herself trapped in her private elevator while a trio of criminals stalk her outside.

The Wizard of Oz (1939)

9 *Type:* _____

Judy Garland gives a dazzling performance in this much-loved movie. She is young Dorothy who is knocked unconscious when a tornado rips through her Kansas farmhouse and who wakes up in the Technicolour world of Oz (the film starts in black and white). A perfect MGM produotion with imaginative sets, photography, costumes and make-up. The classic Harold Arlen/ E Y Harburg songs include *Follow the Yellow Brick Road* and the Oscar-winning *Over the Rainbow*.

Big Business (1988)

10 *Type:* _____

Two sets of identical twins, accidentally separated and switched at birth, meet up years later in New York when one set arrives for a showdown with the corporation that's going to erase their little home town, only to find that the other set of girls is in charge of the company. Excellent performances from Bette Midler and Lily Tomlin. The script is a bit contrived, but there are a lot of laughs.

Who's afraid of Virginia Woolf? (1966)

11 *Type:* _____

Two couples engage in a complex session of all-night conversation that leads to much bitterness and recrimination. Richard Burton and Elizabeth Taylor were never better together than in this totally absorbing but ultimately depressing film.

Ice Castles (1978)

12 *Type:* _____

Tear-jerking romance about a young couple who meet on an ice rink and quickly fall in love. Both find fame and fortune on the ice – he as a professional hockey player, she as an Olympic champion dancer – but tragedy strikes when she becomes blind.

Fantastic Voyage (1966)

13 *Type:* _____

When a famous scientist is shot, a highly experimental technique is used in order to save him. A medical team is placed aboard a submarine, reduced to microscopic size and injected into his bloodstream to remove a blood clot on his brain. An interesting film with excellent special effects.

The Lady and the Tramp
(1955)

14 *Type:* _____

One of Disney's most delightful animated films, in which a pedigree dog runs away from home after the arrival of a baby makes her feel unwanted. She soon meets up with a stray who lives by his wits. The two dogs survive various hazards and win through in the end, when they prove their worth by rescuing the baby. The first Disney film in Cinemascope. Songs are by Peggy Lee and Sonny Burke.

Curse II: The Bite (1988)

15 *Type:* _____

A nest of snakes are infected by radiation and turned into deadly squirming monsters. Anyone they bite is transformed into a terrible mutant beast which will kill you first chance it gets. Frivolous but entertaining monster film.

Other forms of entertainment

Here are some other forms of entertainment. Put them in order 1–8,
starting with your favourite.

going to a disco
going to a nightclub
going to a party
going to a pop concert
going to a restaurant
going to the ballet
going to the circus
going to the funfair
going to the opera
going to the races

going to the zoo
listening to a choir
listening to the radio
playing bingo
playing bridge
playing golf
playing pool
playing squash
watching football
watching television

1 _____

2 _____

3 _____

4 _____

5 _____

6 _____

7 _____

8 _____

When you have finished, compare your choices with those of someone
else in the class. Are there any other forms of entertainment you like
that are not in the list?

Phrasal verbs

1 *Match up the phrasal verbs (1–10) with their meanings (a–j).*
Write your answers in the boxes at the bottom of the page.

1 break up		a not punish, allow to go free
2 bring up		b start a new hobby, pastime
3 cut off		c stop doing something (e.g. smoking)
4 give up		d stop for the holidays (schools)
5 go off		e increase (in weight)
6 let off		f go bad (food)
7 look after		g raise (children, animals)
8 put on		h solve (a problem), calculate
9 take up		i be disconnected (telephone)
10 work out		j care for, take care of

1	2	3	4	5	6	7	8	9	10

2 *Now complete the following dialogues with a suitable phrasal verb. Choose from the above list and make any necessary changes.*

1 A: Would you like a cigarette, John?
   B: No, thanks. I've _____ them _____.

2 A: These trousers don't fit!
   B: I'm not surprised. You've _____ at least two kilos since you last wore them.

3 A: Is that Peter's mother over there?
   B: No, it's his aunt. She _____ him _____ actually. His parents died when he was two.

4 A: What's the answer to question 25?
   B: I'm not going to tell you the answer. _____ it _____ yourself!

5 A: When does your school _____?
   B: July 24th, I think.

6 A: Did Mr Bryant punish you for not doing your homework?
   B: No, he _____ me _____ this time.

7 A: Did Dawn say when she was arriving?
   B: No. We were _____ before she had a chance to tell me.

8 A: I'd like to go to the party, but I can't find a baby-sitter for Jamie.
   B: Don't worry, Pauline. I'll _____ him for you.

9 A: You're looking very fit these days, Harold.
   B: Yes, I'm a new man, Peter, since I _____ jogging. You should try it some time.

10 A: Don't eat that cheese!
   B: Why not?
   A: Because it has _____.

Check 1

This is a check to see how many words you can remember from Section One, Section Two and Section Three. Try to do it without looking back at the previous pages.

1 She had the job before me. She's my _____.

   (a) colleague   (b) successor   (c) opponent   (d) predecessor

2 How might a person feel if he or she looked down from a high building?

   (a) relieved   (b) lonely   (c) giddy   (d) restless

3 Which of the following people works with figures?

   (a) a diver   (b) an accountant   (c) a barrister   (d) a caretaker

4 Which of the following people would you probably know least well?

   (a) your fiancée   (b) your landlord   (c) your twin

   (d) your partner

5 What's a warden in charge of?

   (a) an old people's home   (b) a school   (c) a hospital

   (d) a museum

6 She's always on time. She's very _____.

   (a) affectionate   (b) well-behaved   (c) punctual   (d) frank

7 Which of the following is found inside a car?

   (a) a boot   (b) a wing mirror   (c) a windscreen wiper

   (d) a clutch

8 What's the area at the side of a motorway called, where you can stop if your car breaks down?

   (a) the hard shoulder   (b) the verge   (c) a lay-by   (d) a slip road

9 What does this sign mean?

   (a) Give way   (c) One-way street

   (b) No overtaking   (d) Road works

10 Which of the following wouldn't you normally find on a road?

(a) a coach   (b) a barge   (c) a dustcart   (d) a scooter

11 In each of the following groups of four words, one does not fit in. <u>Underline</u> the word and try to say why it is different from the rest.

(a) boarding pass, Gate 15, buffet car, check in

(b) big-headed, bossy, cheerful, greedy

(c) chalet, youth hostel, guest house, package tour

(d) Australian, English, Spanish, Flemish

(e) flute, cello, oboe, trombone

12 There are fifteen words hidden in the following word square. They are all forms of transport. See how many you can find. You can read vertically (*5 words*), horizontally (*6 words*) or diagonally (*4 words*).

```
A  T  B  O  D  C  I  M  S  E  B  R  O  W  F  J
H  F  A  M  B  U  L  A  N  C  E  L  V  D  B  I
S  D  N  K  I  A  F  K  E  E  L  T  H  A  I  M
C  I  G  P  C  H  B  E  S  U  L  J  R  M  N  O
L  N  E  R  Y  N  I  U  G  M  T  O  D  A  P  R
N  G  A  Y  C  F  A  R  S  Q  A  R  S  C  I  U
C  H  C  A  L  S  K  B  I  S  X  E  N  H  K  N
S  Y  N  C  E  B  J  G  A  L  I  N  E  R  D  P
O  R  F  H  P  G  B  A  D  E  P  L  U  H  A  M
C  E  L  T  C  F  I  R  E  E  N  G  I  N  E  U
A  G  L  O  R  R  Y  N  T  R  I  M  E  V  E  G
N  I  B  A  C  K  C  R  E  T  R  Y  O  K  L  E
O  M  O  T  O  R  B  I  K  E  D  I  D  P  A  L
E  F  K  S  B  O  I  W  E  L  H  A  R  M  E  N
B  A  S  H  O  V  E  R  C  R  A  F  T  B  E  D
I  V  O  W  S  A  L  E  S  B  T  O  O  D  T  H
```

13 Read the following sentences and try to work out what the missing words are. To help you, the first and last letters of the words are given.

(a) He rents a room at our house. He is our l____r.

(b) Both her parents have died. She's an o____n.

(c) He never remembers anything. He's so f_____l.

(d) My neighbour has just bought a new car. I feel so e____s.

(e) She looks after our daughter. She's our c_____r.

(f) Are you tired, Dorothy? You keep y____g!

(g) Babies always c___l before they learn to walk.

(h) Don't throw your rubbish on the pavement. Use the l____r b_n.

(i) A l___l c_____g is where a road crosses a railway line.

(j) The car in front was going so slowly that he decided to o_____e it.

14 Match the words on the left with the ones on the right. Draw lines between the correct pairs.

a bachelor	will inherit
a celebrity	dislikes foreigners
an employee	is famous
an heir	is disabled or ill
an invalid	never eats meat
an optimist	has left his or her country
a racist	looks on the bright side of life
a refugee	no longer has a husband
a vegetarian	is not married
a widow	works for someone

74

15 Say whether the following sentences are correct (C) or incorrect (I)?
  (a) She has never been married. She's a **spinster**.
  (b) He was the only person who died in the crash. He was the only **survivor**.
  (c) Someone who is **skinny** is very thin.
  (d) She hates meeting people or going to parties. She's very **self-confident**.
  (e) He arranges funerals. He's an **undertaker**.
  (f) The **governor** is the person in charge of a newspaper.
  (g) You close both eyes when you **wink**.
  (h) All the meals and entertainment are included in the price at a **holiday camp**.
  (i) An **itinerary** is a plan of a journey.
  (j) At the theatre an **usher** tells actors their lines if they forget them.

16 Look at the picture, then write the missing words in the description below. To help you, the first letter of each missing word is given.

She is an a_____,

d_____-s_____ woman in

her e_____

thirties. She is of

m_____ b_____ and

a_____ a_____ h_____.

She has s_____-l_____

black hair, with a f_____.

17 In the following extract from a holiday brochure the lines are mixed up. Put them in the right order 1–13. Number 1 has been done for you.

____   resorts on the south-east and north-west coasts. The

____   lively sun- and fun-filled holiday, then Ibiza is the place

____   island is also full of sandy beaches with all the usual

____   anywhere in the Mediterranean. If you're looking for a

____   is a major holiday destination, popular with fun-seekers

__1__   Known as 'Isla Blanca', the White Island, Ibiza's beauty

____   of all ages — most of them concentrated on the beach

____   villages, shady olive groves and pine-clad mountains. The

18 Complete the following dialogues with a suitable phrasal verb. The words in brackets after each dialogue should help you.

(a) A: What time did Pete finally _____? *(arrive)*

     B: Just after 11.30.

(b) A: What's the French word for 'happy'?

     B: I haven't a clue. Why don't you _____ it _____ in a dictionary? *(try to find its meaning)*

(c) A: Do you think I've _____ weight, Pam? *(gained)*

     B: Well, maybe a little bit.

(d) A: You're late!

     B: I'm sorry. The bus _____ on the way here. *(stopped working)*

(e) A: Are you going to Mark's party on Friday?

     B: Haven't you heard? He's _____ it _____. *(cancelled it)*

(f) A: What are you going to do when you retire?

     B: Oh, I'll probably _____ painting. *(start painting as a hobby)*

(g) A: What do you think of this tie?

     B: It's all right. But it doesn't _____ your jacket. *(match)*

(h) A: Aren't you on holiday yet?

B: No, our school doesn't _____ until next week. *(close)*

(i) A: I'd like to join the library, please.

B: Certainly. Just _____ this form. *(complete)*

(j) A: Cigarette, Mandy?

B: No, thanks. I _____ smoking two months ago. *(stopped)*

19 Look at the drawing of the theatre below, then write the numbers 1–12 next to the following words.

aisle	curtain	orchestra pit	stage
box office	dressing-room	programme	stalls
circle/balcony	foyer	row	wings

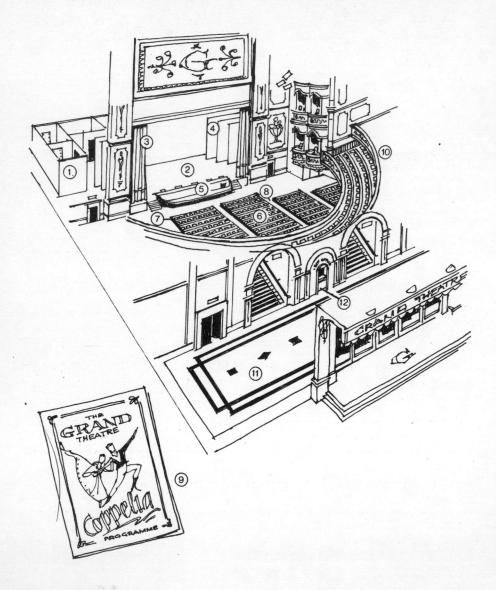

20 Here are thirty words in alphabetical order. Place each word
under the correct heading (*5 words under each*).

accordion	carriage	inter-city	pillar box
airport	check-in desk	express	platform
baggage	cliff	kerb	restaurant car
reclaim	deck-chair	lamp-post	roundabout
beach	departure	motorway	synthesizer
boarding pass	lounge	outside lane	ticket collector
bongoes	diversion	pavement	tuba
building site	harp	pier	wave
by-pass			

Musical instruments

_____

_____

_____

_____

_____

At the seaside

_____

_____

_____

_____

_____

In the town

_____

_____

_____

_____

_____

Travelling by road

_____

_____

_____

_____

_____

Travelling by plane

_____

_____

_____

_____

_____

Travelling by train

_____

_____

_____

_____

_____

21   Look at the drawings of a car below and complete the crossword.

Key.
1A (3) = 1 Across, 3 letters in the word
3D (3, 6) = 3 Down, two words of 3 and 6 letters each

(NOTE: In crosswords two words are written together as one word.)

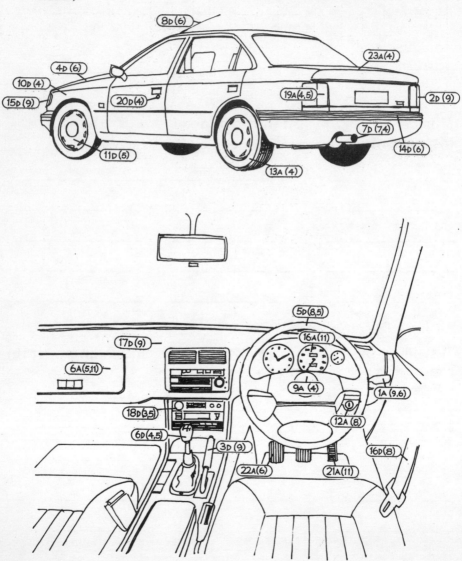

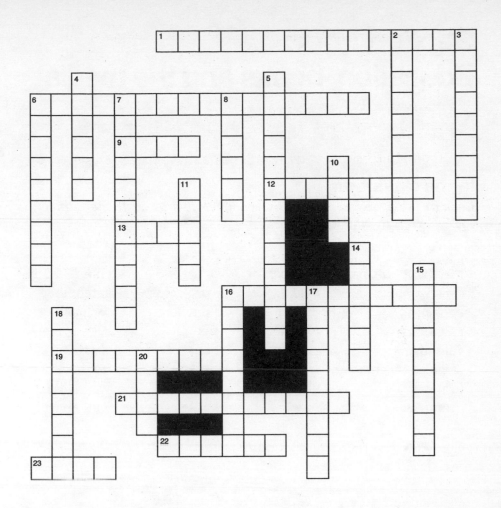

Section Four:
Education, books and the media

In the classroom

Look at the drawing of the classroom below and write the numbers 1–28 next to the following words.

biro/ballpoint pen	cupboard	overhead	ruler
(black)board	desk	projector	satchel/
bookcase	duster	pencil	schoolbag
calculator	exercise	pencil	set square
calendar	book	sharpener	shelf
(a piece of) chalk	felt-tip pen	protractor	textbook
(a pair of)	globe	pupil	timetable
compasses	glue	rubber	wall chart

British schools and institutions

Read the definitions below and write the numbers 1–18 next to the following words.

boarding school	primary school
co-educational school	private school
College of Further Education	public school
comprehensive school	secondary school
evening classes	Sixth-Form College
nursery school	state school
playschool	Teacher Training College
Polytechnic	The Open University
prep school	university

1 This is a school which is run by the government and where education is free.

2 This is a school which is not supported by government money and where parents have to pay for their children's education. It is sometimes called an independent school.

3 This is the school a child attends from the age of 5 to the age of 11.

4 This is a school for children between 3 and 5 years of age. Most of them are run by local education authorities.

5 This is an institution where students study for degrees and where academic research is done. The most famous ones are Oxford and Cambridge.

6 This is the school a child attends after the age of 11 and until he or she is 16 or 18.

7 This is similar to a nursery school but is not usually run by the local education authority. It is an informal school where children learn to play with other children as well as learning other things through play rather than formal lessons.

8 This is usually a private school where the pupils live during the term and only go home to their parents during the holidays.

9 This is the most common type of state secondary school where pupils of all abilities and backgrounds are taught together.

10 This is a private school for pupils up to the age of 13, where they are made ready (or prepared) to attend a school for older pupils, usually a public school.

11 This college specializes in training people to become teachers.

12 This is a college for people who have left school and want more qualifications at a lower level than a degree. Here, the courses are often linked to some kind of practical training, for example, typing, hairdressing, etc.

13 This is a special type of university, open to everyone, which uses radio and television for teaching and the students' work is sent to them by post.

14 These are courses for adults held in most towns — usually in the evenings — where students, for a small fee, study a variety of things, from French to flower arranging.

15 This is a college which specializes in preparing people for particular jobs in science, industry, etc.

16 This is a private school which provides secondary education for pupils between the ages of 13 and 18. Usually it has a long tradition and fees are expensive. Two of the most famous ones are Eton and Harrow.

17 This is a school for pupils between the ages of 16 and 18, who are preparing to take their A-level examination.

18 This is a school where boys and girls are taught together in the same buildings and classrooms.

Follow up

Now place the following words in the correct places in the chart below.

College of Further Education, comprehensive school, nursery school, playschool, Polytechnic, prep school, primary school, public school, Sixth-Form College, Teacher Training College, university

Schools for children under 5	
State schools (5–18)	
Private schools (5–18)	
Higher education (people who have left school)	

Who's who in education

Match the people (1–15) on the left with a definition (a–o) from the right. Write your answers in the boxes at the top of the next page.

1 apprentice	a A person (usually a child) who attends a school.
2 caretaker	
3 expert	b A student who has completed a first degree course at a university or college.
4 governor	c *Either* a teacher at a university who teaches small groups of students *or* someone who privately teaches one pupil or a small group of pupils, often at home.
5 graduate	
6 headteacher	
7 lecturer	d A person who teaches at a college or university.
8 principal	
9 pupil	e A young person who works for a number of years with someone – usually for low wages – in order to learn their skills, e.g. a hairdresser.
10 scholar	
11 staff	
12 student	f The person in charge of a university.
13 tutor	g A person who studies an academic subject, e.g. Greek, and knows a lot about it.
14 undergraduate	h A person who is very skilled at doing something or who knows a lot about a subject.
15 vice-chancellor	

i All the people who work at a school, college or university.

j A person who is a member of the committee which controls a school.

k A student at a college or university who is studying for his or her first degree.

l The person in charge of a school or college.

m The person in charge of a school.

n The person who looks after a school and is responsible for repairs, cleaning, etc.

o A person who is studying at a college or university.

1	2	3	4	5	6	7	8	9	10	11	12	13	14	15

Verbs to do with education

Write the missing verbs in the sentences below. Choose from the following list. Make changes where necessary.

attend	learn (something)	punish
behave	by heart	recite
do one's homework	leave school	revise
enrol	pass	sit/take (an exam)
expel	play truant	specialize
fail	praise	study
		test

1 She _____ at 16 to go and work in her cousin's shop.

2 The headteacher _____ the school football team for doing so well in the local Cup.

3 I can't come out tonight, I'm afraid. I've got to _____ for a test tomorrow.

4 Children from the age of 5 to 11 usually _____ a primary school.

5 None of the teachers could control the boy. When he finally tried to set fire to the school, the headteacher was forced to _____ him. Since he has gone, things have been a lot more peaceful.

6 When he went to the Sixth-Form College he decided to _____ in languages.

7 This course is very popular. If you want a place on it you'd better _____ today.

8 The teacher told the class that their homework was to _____ a poem _____ and that she would ask them to _____ it in class the following week.

9 She went to university to _____ mathematics.

10 In a mixed class, boys generally _____ worse than girls.

11 He was very upset when he _____ his exams, especially as he thought he had done so well.

12 She spends at least two hours every night _____ her _____.

13 He was a very strict teacher and always _____ his pupils if they forgot to do their homework or misbehaved in class.

14 We are going to _____ the Cambridge First Certificate examination at the end of next month.

15 'At the end of the term we shall _____ you all to find out how good you are in English and maths,' the teacher told the class.

16 To _____ means to stay away from school without permission.

17 She was extremely intelligent and found it very easy to _____ all her exams.

Other useful words to do with education

Write the missing words in the sentences below. Choose from the following:

absent	detention	playground	staff-room
academic	form	present	subjects
assignment	gymnasium	register	terms
compulsory	lecture	scholarship	tutorial
course	mark	seminar	vacation
deputy head			

1 My daughter is in the fifth _____ of the local comprehensive school.

2 The teacher gave her a very high _____ for her essay.

3 If you get a _____ to a school or university, your studies are paid for by the school or university or some other organization.

4 My favourite _____ at school were English, art and music.

5 A teacher usually fills in a _____ every day to show which children are _____ (at school) and which children are _____ (not there).

6 When he was a student at university he used to work during the summer _____ as a waiter.

7 If the headteacher is ill or away, the _____ usually takes over the running of the school.

8 A _____ is when a teacher at a university or college gives a prepared talk to a group of students.

9 You don't usually talk about homework at university. You use the word _____ instead.

10 The _____ is where teachers in a school relax, prepare their lessons, mark their books, etc.

11 Education in Britain is _____ between the ages of 5 and 16.

12 The teacher punished the child by putting her in _____, that is, she was made to stay after school and do extra work.

13 A _____ is when a teacher at a university or college discusses a subject with a group of students.

14 In Britain, the school or _____ year starts in September and ends in July. It is divided into three _____.

15 She went on a _____ to learn about word-processing.

16 During the break, the children were made to go out into the _____.

17 A _____ is when a teacher at a university or college gives an individual lesson to one or more students.

18 We usually have our physical education lessons in the _____.

Types of book

Read the definitions below of different types of book and then write the numbers 1–24 next to the following words.

anthology	directory	paperback
atlas	encyclopedia	poetry book
autobiography	fiction	reference book
best seller	guidebook	romantic novel
biography	hardback	science fiction novel
book of fairy tales	manual	textbook
cookery book	memoirs	thriller
dictionary	non-fiction	whodunnit

1 A book or a set of books in which facts are arranged for reference, usually in alphabetical order. If you want information about something, you ought to be able to find it in this book.

2 A book in which the words of a language are listed in alphabetical order, with their meanings and pronunciations.

3 A book which gives you information about how to do something, especially how a machine works.

4 Books about imaginary people and events.

5 A book which is about a murder and in which the identity of the murderer is kept a secret until the end.

6 A book full of maps.

7 Writing that gives information or is about real things and events rather than imaginary ones. Generally speaking, any literature which is not poetry, plays, stories and novels.

8 An account of a person's life written by that person.

9 A book which gives a list of people's names, addresses, telephone numbers, etc. usually arranged in alphabetical order.

10 A book for the study of a particular subject, e.g. English or mathematics, which is used by students, especially in schools.

11 A book with a thin, card cover.

12 A book full of recipes and information on how to prepare and cook food.
13 A book which tells an exciting story about dangerous, frightening or mysterious events.
14 A collection of poems or other pieces of writing by different writers, published together in one book.
15 A book for tourists which gives information about a town, area or country.
16 Similar to an autobiography, but often about someone's experiences, especially someone who has been active in politics or war.
17 A novel which deals mainly with love and romance and which usually has a happy ending.
18 A book which is very popular and has sold a large number of copies.
19 A book for children with stories about magical events and imaginary creatures such as fairies.
20 A novel about events that take place in the future or in other parts of the universe.
21 A book with a strong, stiff cover.
22 A book full of poems.
23 An account of a person's life written by someone else.
24 A book, such as a dictionary or encyclopedia, that you look at when you need information, rather than a book you read from beginning to end.

Follow up

Now see if you can work out what types of book the following extracts are taken from.

1 Once upon a time there was a giant who lived in a cave in the Blue Mountains.

2 **TRANSMITTING A FAX MESSAGE**
   Document loading
   - Place the document (max. 20 pages) FACE DOWN on to the document feeder tray.
   - Adjust paper guides to suit paper width.

3 She was born in a small Welsh village on December 10th, 1944. The youngest of three children, even from an early age she showed the talent that would one day take her to Hollywood.

4 New Zealand is a land of contrasts. Tropical rain forests, alpine waterfalls, barren semi-deserts, green farmland meadows, golden sun-drenched beaches, stormy coasts and wide flat plains are seen almost side by side.

5 Set the oven to 150°. Rub a little butter round the inside of a large cake tin, 25 cm across. Put a piece of buttered paper on the bottom of the cake tin.

6 Samantha gazed lovingly into Tom's eyes and whispered gently, 'Tom, I love you. You're the only man I've ever really loved.'

7 It was the year 2478 and exactly fifty years since the Second Galactic War.

8 My childhood, as far as I remember, was a very happy one. I was born in the small Sussex village of Westfield in the days when the sight of a car going through the village would be a cause of excitement and wonder.

9 The hand that signed the paper felled a city;
   Five sovereign fingers taxed the breath,
   Doubled the globe of dead and halved a country;
   These five kings did a king to death.

10 'I never murdered him, I tell you. It's not true!'

'I know that, sir. I've known it all along,' Inspector Bates said quietly. 'You know that too, don't you Mr Pike?'

'What? What on earth are you talking about?'

'The murderer couldn't have been your cousin, Mr Pike, could he? Because it was you!'

11 He ran along the aisle and paused, staring down at the body. It was then, sensing too late that something was very wrong indeed, that he reached for the Webley revolver in his holster.

Devlin stepped out, the silenced Walther in his left hand. 'I wouldn't do that, son. This thing makes no more noise than you or me coughing. Now turn round.'

12 **normal**/ no:ml/

ADJ Something that is **normal** is usual and ordinary, and what people expect. *Under **normal** circumstances only a small fraction of the population is affected... Washington must first lift economic sanctions and restore **normal** relations... This is a perfectly **normal** baby.*

Parts of a book

Write the missing words in the drawing and sentences below. Choose from the following:

acknowledgements	contents	illustrations
appendix	cover	index
bibliography	footnote	jacket
blurb	foreword	preface
chapter	glossary	title

1 _____

2 _____

3 _____

4 A _____ is a list of the books and articles that were used in the preparation of a book. It usually appears at the end.

5 The _____ are the photographs or drawings that are found in a book.

6 The _____ at the beginning or end of a book are where the author thanks everyone who has helped him or her, plus who supplied photographs, etc.

7 A _____ is an introduction at the beginning of a book, which explains what the book is about or why it was written.

8 A _____ is one of the parts that a book is divided into. It is sometimes given a number or a title.

9 An _____ to a book is extra information that is placed after the end of the main text.

10 A _____ is a preface in which someone who knows the writer and his or her work says something about them.

11 An _____ is an alphabetical list that is sometimes printed at the back of a book which has the names, subjects, etc. mentioned in the book and the pages where they can be found.

12 The _____ is a list at the beginning of a book saying what it contains.

13 The _____ is an alphabetical list of the special or technical words used in a book, with explanations of their meanings.

14 A _____ is a note at the bottom of a page in a book which gives the reader more information about something that is mentioned on the page.

15 The _____ is a short description by the publisher of the contents of a book, printed on its paper cover or in advertisements.

The media: Television
Types of programme
Here is a list of the most common types of TV programme and what sort of programme they are.

Programme type	Description
1 chat show	
2 children's programme	A programme suitable for children and young people.
3 comedy series (sitcom)	
4 detective series	
5 documentary	
6 drama series	
7 educational programme	A programme intended to teach or educate viewers.
8 food programme	A programme about food.
9 music programme	A programme about music (pop, classical).
10 nature programme	
11 news and current affairs programmes	Daily news broadcasts plus programmes dealing with things that are happening in the world today.
12 play	
13 quiz show	
14 soap opera	
15 sports programme	A programme about sport (football, the Olympic Games, etc.).
16 travel programme	
17 TV film	A film specially made for television.

Unfortunately, some descriptions are missing. Choose from the following descriptions and write the letter (a–j) next to the correct programme.

a   A complete drama, performed by actors.

b   A programme that presents facts and information about a particular subject.

c   A programme that deals with some aspect of travelling, e.g. a programme that looks at places the viewers could go to on holiday.

d   A programme where a host talks to a number of guests, often famous actors, singers, politicians, writers, etc.

e   A programme where individuals compete against each other, usually by answering questions. Often there are prizes to be won.

f   A programme which shows the same set of characters in each episode, in amusing situations that are often similar to everyday life, e.g. *Fawlty Towers*, which starred John Cleese as the owner of a small hotel in Torquay.

g   A programme that shows films of how animals, fish, birds, etc., live.

h   A very popular type of series which is usually based on the daily lives of a family or community, e.g. *Coronation Street, Eastenders*.

i   Individual plays featuring the same set of characters. Each episode is either complete in itself or it can be a long story divided into a number of separate episodes.

j   A series where the main character, usually a policeman or detective, solves a crime, e.g. *Maigret, Inspector Morse*.

Follow up

Using the above information, see if you can work out what sort of programmes the following are.

Work is a Four-Letter Word
A six-part series to help improve speaking and writing skills.
1: How to use the phone to best advantage.

1 _____

Challenge of the Seas
A look at the dolphins and crocodiles which inhabit Florida Bay.

2 _____

40 minutes
The programme follows 46 women recruits in an army training camp in Kapooka, Australia, as they undergo the painful transformation from civilian to soldier.

3 _____

Bruce Springsteen: Plugged
A rare TV appearance in Los Angeles during Bruce Springsteen's world tour in which he performs material spanning from his early days through to his recent albums.

4 _____

The Inspector Alleyn Mysteries
The Nursing Home Murder
A prominent cabinet minister dies as the result of an operation, and his wife insists that it was murder. Alleyn is called in but can he calm her fears?

5 _____

King of the Road
A daily programme visiting fascinating towns and cities in the UK, meeting local 'characters' and finding places of interest. Today, Ross King and Anna Walker visit Bradford in Yorkshire.

6 _____

Out of Westminster
The weekly coverage of Parliament and the wider political scene.

7 _____

Lucky Ladders
The word association game hosted by Lennie Bennett.

8 _____

Masterchef
Cardiff is the home to all three contestants in tonight's heat to find the best amateur chef in Great Britain.

9 _____

Heartbeat
Series set in the 60s about a young policeman, starring **Nick Berry** and **Niamh Cusak**.
Manhunt. Returning late to Aidensfield, Nick makes a routine call to the pub and finds himself in unexpected company. It is the start of a strange and, for some, terrifying night.

10 _____

The media: Newspapers
Useful words to do with newspapers
Write the missing words in the sentences below. Choose from the following:

advertisements	comic strip	letters page
article	crossword	obituary
caption	editor	popular papers
correspondent	editorial	quality papers
circulation	feature	reporter
classified	gossip column	review
advertisements	headline	sports pages
colour supplement	horoscope	tabloid
column	journalist	weather forecast

1 There was a large _____ on the front page which said
EARTHQUAKE SHAKES TOKYO.
2 The person in charge of a newspaper is called the _____.
3 Since the newspaper changed owners, its _____ has
increased by nearly 10,000 copies a month.
4 If you have strong views about something, you can always make
them known by writing to the _____ .
5 After reading the front page I always turn to the _____
to find out the latest football results.
6 A story or report written for a newspaper is called an
_____.
7 A large proportion of a newspaper's income comes from
_____, especially full-page ones.
8 He always read his _____ every morning to find out
what was going to happen to him that day – especially to find out
if he was going to win money or meet an exciting stranger.
9 Before we go for our picnic this afternoon, we'd better check the
_____. There's no point in going if it's going to rain.

10 In Britain, the national newspapers can be divided into _____, such as *The Times* and the *Daily Telegraph*, which report the news seriously and thoroughly, and the _____, such as *The Sun* and the *Daily Mirror*, which go in for sensational news and use lots of pictures, often of girls.

11 Editors usually think very carefully about what _____ to write under a photograph.

12 A _____ is a set of drawings telling a story, often humorous. There are usually words showing the speech of the characters in the story.

13 There was not enough room on the front page for the complete article, so it was continued on page 2 _____ 4.

14 You read the _____ to find out about the private lives (and scandals) of famous people.

15 Many Sunday newspapers include free a special magazine to read called a _____.

16 An _____ is a piece of writing about the character and achievements of someone who has just died.

17 For many years before returning to Britain he worked as a foreign _____ in Paris and Turkey.

18 There was a very interesting _____ today, giving the newspaper's opinion of the government's new plans for the health service.

19 If you want to buy a new car, rent a flat or buy a second-hand bed, then you might be able to find something in the _____.

20 I prefer reading _____ newspapers as they are smaller and easier to handle. Reading newspapers like *The Times* makes my arms ache after a while.

21 The new television series got a very bad _____ in today's newspaper. It was described as 'the worst series the BBC has ever made'.

22 A person who writes for a newspaper is called a _____ or a _____.

23 All this week the newspaper is running a special _____
on love and marriage.

24 I've just got one word left to complete this _____. It's got six
letters and the clue is 'Shakespearean romantic heroine'.

Follow up

*Using the words in the list on page 101, try to decide what the extracts
below are or where in a newspaper you would find them.*

1 Eastern Scotland and England will be cloudy at times, but
remaining areas will see plenty of sunshine.

2 £500 for parking on yellow lines

3 I am delighted to report that Prince Edward is keeping himself
busy between theatrical engagements. Tonight he will be in the
company of the Samoan rugby team at the Groucho Club in Soho.

4 Can the professional reputation of such actors as Stephanie
Beacham and John Standing survive such hilarious rubbish as
Riders (ITV)? Why on earth did director Gabrielle Beaumont
pass such wooden performances?

5 If John Major does not want to restrict the traditional liberty of
our citizens with the issue of ID cards, why doesn't he obstruct
Irish people travelling to and from this country by making them
apply for visas? This way, a check could be made on those
suspected of terrorism more easily.

Mrs S. Austin
Brighton, East Sussex

6 During her career, she appeared with most of the Hollywood
greats, but it wasn't until 1992 that she won her first and only
Oscar. She leaves a husband and three daughters.

7 **FOUND**: purse and cash in city centre, 28th April. Tel. 290734, evenings.

WANTED: Antique and old-fashioned furniture for the export market. Home clearance specialist, established 30 years. Tel 737542 for an offer you can't refuse.

TV VIDEO Sales and Service. Free estimates. White Electronics. Tel. 844521.

8 Today you can do anything you set your mind to. Romance is in the air and the end of the week is a good time for investing money.

9 Owls Cup fears as Wilson limps out

Sheff Wed 1 Leeds 1

David Hirst scored a goal in the last minute to equalize as he warmed up for Wembley last night, but there was a scare for Sheffield Wednesday team-mate Danny Wilson.

10

11 RIVALS: Richard Wilson (left) as Meldrew and Lovejoy star Ian McShane (right).

12 DOWN

4 Don't go along with rubbish! (4)

A newspaper article

The following newspaper article is mixed up. See if you can sort it out. Number the lines 1–18. Three of the numbers have already been filled in.

Barefoot chase after porch theft

By Terry Crockford

___ Road house when he heard a knock at the door and saw

___ at least 20 pounds each. I couldn't get near him but as he got

___ One of the grey stone ornaments, measuring about 14 inches

_1_ Barefoot and wearing only pyjamas and a robe, a man from

___ worth around £50.

___ into a car I shouted to a man on a bike ahead of me to get his

___ tration of the red Fiesta getaway car.

_7_ "He went off down the street, an ornament in each hand,

___ Jim Rutherford was on the phone in the bedroom of his Cecil

___ Gowerton dashed 400 yards down a street after a man who stole

___ "He must have been a strong lad because these things weigh

___ number."

___ woman on a bench feeding squirrels. The pair is said to be

___ his garden ornaments.

_13_ Police were called and checks are being made on the regis-

___ with me racing after him," said Jim.

___ tall, depicts a man sitting on a bench while the other is of a

___ someone making off with two stone ornaments from the porch.

(From *South Wales Evening Post*, May 5, 1993)

Phrasal verbs

1 *Match the phrasal verbs (1–10) with their meanings (a–j). Write your answers in the boxes at the bottom of the page.*

1 come across

2 come round

3 fall out

4 get over (something)

5 look at

6 look for

7 look up to

8 pick up

9 take after

10 take off

a examine, consider

b learn (how to do something, a language)

c remove (clothing)

d find by accident

e respect, admire

f quarrel, stop being friends

g resemble, look like, be like (someone)

h regain consciousness (after fainting)

i try to find

j recover from something (e.g. an illness, disaster, etc.)

1	2	3	4	5	6	7	8	9	10

2 *Now complete the following dialogues with a suitable phrasal verb. Choose from the list on the previous page and make any necessary changes.*

1 A: How's your father?

   B: Not too good, I'm afraid. He still hasn't _____ the death of my mother.

2 A: Are there any politicians you _____?

   B: Not these days. But I used to admire Margaret Thatcher.

3 A: Where on earth did you get this old photo?

   B: Oh, I _____ it when I was tidying up the other day.

4 A: It's very hot in here!

   B: Well, _____ your jacket, then.

5 A: Could you _____ this please, Jill? Just to make sure I haven't made any mistakes.

   B: Yes, of course. Just leave it on my desk.

6 A: I didn't know you could speak Spanish, Pam.

   B: Didn't you? Oh, I _____ it _____ when I worked as a tour guide on the Costa Brava.

7 A: What did you do when she fainted?

   B: I threw some water over her face and she _____ .

8 A: Your daughter's very musical, Mrs Kimble.

   B: Yes, I know. She _____ her father. He's a musician.

9 A: Aren't you speaking to Colin these days?

   B: No, we _____ last week and haven't spoken to each other since.

10 A: I can't find that book Tom lent me.

   B: Don't worry, I'll help you to _____ it.

Section Five: Word-building

Prefixes 1

You can change the meaning of a word in English by placing a prefix (un-, im-, dis-, etc.) in front of it.

Add a prefix (dis-, in-, ir-, mis- or re-) to the following root words, then fill the gaps in the sentences below.

advantage	dependent	like	responsible
agree	formal	print	write
correct	honest		

1 It was very _____ of her to cheat in the examination.

2 It was very _____ of you to go away for the weekend without telling your parents where you were.

3 It is a great _____ nowadays not to be able to drive – especially when applying for a job.

4 You don't need to wear a suit or a jacket; it's going to be a very _____ party.

5 I'm not very happy with this essay. I think I'll _____ it.

6 17 plus 18 doesn't make 46. That's _____. The right answer is 35.

7 There was an amusing _____ in today's newspaper. Instead of saying 'The choir often sings for charity' it said, 'The choir often sins for charity'.

8 This year our country will have been _____ for 40 years.

9 'I think shops should be closed on Sundays.'

'I _____! I think they should be open seven days a week.'

10 I _____ all animals – especially dogs. My sister, on the other hand, loves them.

Prefixes 2

Add a prefix (il-, im-, non- or un-) to the following root words, then fill the gaps in the sentences below.

certain	friendly	polite	true
comfortable	legal	possible	violence
employed	patient		

1 I would never make a good teacher – I'm far too _____.

2 Most modern cities are lonely, dangerous and rather _____ places.

3 In Britain it is _____ to drive a car without insurance and road tax.

4 Because of the bad weather it is _____ whether the open-air concert will take place or not.

5 The Indian leader, Gandhi, was a great believer in _____. He believed protests and demonstrations should be peaceful ones.

6 No person can live to the age of 300 – it's _____.

7 Don't believe a word he tells you. It's all _____!

8 Pass me a cushion please, Paul. This chair's very _____.

9 Her children are very _____ and never say 'Please' or 'Thank you'.

10 I've been _____ for three months now. I really must get a job soon.

Follow up

Now decide which prefixes you would put in front of the following words. Put them under the correct heading.

appear	experienced	logical	regular
behave	fiction	loyal	relevant
common	fortunately	lucky	satisfied
complete	happy	mature	smoker
consistent	human	moral	treat
expected	literate	obey	understand
expensive			

dis-	il-
im-	in-
ir-	mis-
non-	un-

Now try writing your own sentences containing some of the above words.

Suffixes: Changing words into nouns for people

You can also change a word by adding a suffix (-al, -ence, -less, -ment, etc.) after it.

Add a suffix to the following words* (-er, -or, -ian or -ist), then fill the gaps in the sentences below.

| art | direct | guitar | manage | politics | terror |
| collect | electric | library | own | survive | write |

1 If you need to find a particular book, the _____ will help you.

2 She was the only _____ of the plane crash. Everyone else was killed.

3 'Would the _____ of the blue Volvo, registration number F679 DEP, please move it as it is blocking the entrance.'

4 There are very few people who have never heard of the Dutch _____ Vincent Van Gough.

5 Alfred Hitchcock is the film _____ I admire most.

6 He had always wanted to be a _____, so we weren't a bit surprised to hear that he had published a novel.

7 Many people consider Margaret Thatcher to be the best British _____ of this century.

8 She could play several musical instruments, but it was as a _____ that she became famous.

9 To prevent a _____ attack, there is always very tight security at international airports.

10 She has been a stamp _____ since she was a child.

11 My son is training to be an _____. That should be handy for us when we rewire our new house.

12 One of the most difficult jobs in the world must be that of _____ of a top football club – especially when the team is playing badly.

* You may have to make small changes, e.g. where the last letter of the root word drops out or changes into another letter

Suffixes: Changing words into adjectives 1

Add a suffix to the following words (-ful, -ing, -less or -y), then fill the gaps in the sentences below.

anger	care	frighten	pain
beauty	doubt	health	use
bore	excite	home	wind

1 Being in a department store when a bomb went off was one of the most _____ experiences of his life. He was terrified.

2 It's no good trying to put your umbrella up – it's far too _____. It will only get blown inside-out.

3 She was a very _____ driver and had never had an accident since she started driving twenty-five years ago.

4 There are still thousands of _____ people in our big cities who are forced to sleep rough every night.

5 My father was really _____ when I told him I had smashed the car. For a minute I thought he was going to hit me.

6 I feel really _____ since I gave up smoking and started jogging.

7 This knife is _____ – it won't cut!

8 It is _____ whether the new Town Hall will be built now, as the local council has run out of money.

9 It was such a _____ TV programme that she fell asleep half-way through it.

10 Nowadays, going to the dentist and having a tooth out is a pretty _____ operation. Most people don't feel a thing.

11 The final of the World Cup in football was a very _____ match. It was only in the very last minute that England scored the winning goal.

12 What a _____ dress you're wearing! It's really gorgeous!

Suffixes: Changing words into adjectives 2

Add a suffix to the following words (-able, -al, -ic, -ive or -ous), then fill the gaps in the sentences below.

accident	centre	create	music
artist	comfort	danger	optimist
attract	courage	fame	rely

1 Our parents wouldn't let us go rock-climbing. They thought it was too _____ and that we might kill ourselves.

2 He was a very _____ person and was always expecting the best to happen.

3 We caught our train at the _____ station.

4 'What sort of a job are you looking for?'
'Oh, something _____ – you know, working in films, television, design, advertising – that sort of thing.'

5 Don't ask James to do it, he's not very _____. The last time we asked him to help us, he didn't even turn up.

6 It was _____! I didn't drop the vase on purpose. It just slipped out of my hand.

7 'Did you sleep well?'
'Oh yes. The bed was really _____.'

8 The Beatles are one of the most _____ pop groups of all time. Very few people have never heard of them.

9 Your daughter's going to be a painter, Mrs Green. She's very _____.

10 Mozart developed his _____ talents at a very young age.

11 The troops were extremely _____ during the battle.

12 'What's the new boss like?'
'She's tall, dark and very _____. She looks more like a film star than a bank manager.'

Suffixes: Changing words into nouns 1

Add a suffix to the following words (-al, -ance, -ence, or -y), then fill the gaps in the sentences below.

absent	differ	important	perform
apologize	difficult	insure	refuse
arrive	discover	intelligent	try

1 I had great _____ in starting the car this morning. There must be something wrong with the battery.

2 I wish I had the body of Mr Universe, the looks of Mel Gibson and the _____ of Albert Einstein.

3 The _____ at the Old Bailey took six weeks. In the end, the jury found him guilty and he was sent to prison for three years.

4 Your behaviour was disgusting last night. I think you owe everyone an _____.

5 'I cannot stress the _____ of passing this exam enough,' the teacher told the class. 'Your whole future may depend on it.'

6 Everyone was shocked at her _____ to attend her son's wedding.

7 The crowd waited excitedly for the _____ of Princess Diana.

8 Countries in the Middle East became rich following the _____ of oil.

9 If pupils in Britain miss school, they are expected to take a letter to their teacher from their parents explaining their _____.

10 Sir Anthony Hopkins was awarded an Oscar for his _____ in *The Silence of the Lambs*.

11 Can you tell the _____ between butter and margarine?

12 _____ companies lost millions of pounds when a hurricane destroyed property all along the south coast.

115

Suffixes: Changing words into nouns 2

Add a suffix to the following words (-age, -ation, -ion, -sion or -tion),
then fill the gaps in the sentences below.

describe	elect	invite	post
discuss	explode	marry	pronounce
educate	invent	mile	suggest

1 Who do you think will win the next _____ – the Conservatives or the Labour party?

2 He knew a lot of grammar and vocabulary, but his _____ was so bad that no one could understand a word he was saying.

3 The _____ of the computer has had an enormous impact on people's lives.

4 You get very good _____ from this car – at least 40 miles to the gallon.

5 'How about going to see Mandy and Nick tonight?'
'No, thank you! Have you forgotten already what happened last time?'
'All right, all right. Forget it! It was only a _____.'

6 _____ in Britain is compulsory between the ages of 5 and 16.

7 This is his second _____. His first wife died in a car crash three years ago.

8 There was a very lively _____ on TV last night about the proposed introduction of identity cards in Britain.

9 It is now confirmed that three people died in yesterday's _____ in a restaurant in Soho. This is the third IRA bombing in London this month.

10 Have you had an _____ to Jill's wedding yet?

11 The police asked the witness for a _____ of the armed robber.

12 The book costs £15 plus £2.50 _____.

116

Suffixes: Changing words into nouns 3

Add a suffix to the following words (-ity, -ment or -ness), then fill the gaps in the sentences below.

active	dark	govern	sad
advertise	disappoint	ill	treat
arrange	equal	popular	weak

1 She found it hard to hide her _____ at not winning an Oscar, as she was the hot favourite to win it.

2 There is far too much _____ in the world today. I wish there was something you could do to make people happier.

3 There was a full-page _____ in today's paper for the new Jaguar car.

4 He has a _____ for cream cakes. He just can't resist eating them.

5 Although it is desirable, I don't think there will ever be true _____ between men and women.

6 She made an _____ to see her bank manager at 11.30 on Friday morning.

7 There was a lot of _____ outside my bedroom window this morning. The noise woke me up.

8 Do you get free dental _____ in your country, or do you have to pay for it?

9 The more unemployment rises, the less popular the _____ gets – especially the Prime Minister.

10 We tried to get home before _____ came, as I hate driving at night.

11 His _____ with television viewers went down enormously after a newspaper published photographs of him beating his dog.

12 'Your _____ is a direct result of smoking,' the doctor told his patient. 'The sooner you stop, the better.'

Changing words into nouns 4 (various endings)

Change the following words into nouns that will fit in the gaps in the sentences below.

angry	die	hot	lose
choose	fly	know	sign
deep	high	long	strong

1 A _____ of foreign languages, especially French and German, is required for this job.

2 The painting looked genuine but the _____ was obviously a forgery. It was spelt 'Piccaso' instead of 'Picasso'.

3 The _____ of the river at this point is over five metres.

4 For the first time in its history, instead of making a huge profit, the company had made a _____ of £10 million.

5 Judo requires both skill and _____.

6 Tea or coffee, Pam? You decide. It's your _____.

7 I could never live in Spain because of the _____. I can't move once the temperature goes over 25°.

8 The _____ of the mountain is approximately 2,000 metres.

9 The workers reacted with _____ and frustration at the news that they were going to close the factory.

10 His sudden _____ from AIDS at the age of 24 came as a great shock to everyone.

11 The width of the room is four metres and its _____ is seven.

12 We arrived early at the airport only to be told that our _____ had been delayed because of ice on the runway.

Changing nouns into adjectives (various endings)

*Fill the gaps in each of the sentences below by changing the nouns printed in **bold** type into adjectives.*

1 **ambition** She was very _____ and hoped to be a top barrister before she was 35.

2 **cloud** I don't think we'll go down to the beach today and sunbathe – it's too _____.

3 **day** *The Times* is perhaps the most famous _____ newspaper in Britain.

4 **help** Thank you for everything you've done. You've been most _____.

5 **hunger** I must eat something soon, I'm so _____!

6 **law** Is it _____ to drive a car when you're 16 in your country?

7 **luck** They were very _____ not to be killed when their car crashed into a lamp-post.

8 **medicine** Before they would offer her the job, she had to agree to have a _____ examination.

9 **mountain** Switzerland and Austria are very _____ countries.

10 **mystery** The police are still looking into the _____ disappearance of the chief cashier shortly after the bank robbery.

11 **nation** Rugby is the _____ sport of Wales.

12 **poison** There is only one _____ snake in Britain – the adder or viper.

13 **profession** You can earn a lot of money nowadays as a _____ footballer.

14 **reason** We decided to take the flat because it was quite big, in a good position and the rent was very _____.

15 **sense** I think the most _____ thing to do is to wait a bit longer before buying your house, just in case prices come down even more.

119

16 **south**   The weather is best in the _____ part of the country.

17 **success**   The song she wrote was so _____ that she decided to give up her job and become a full-time songwriter.

18 **sympath**y   My neighbours were very kind and _____ when my husband died.

19 **taste**   What sort of fish is this? It's completely _____!

20 **use**   A phrasebook is a very _____ thing to have with you when you visit a foreign country.

Changing adjectives into nouns (various endings)

Fill the gaps in each of the sentences below by changing the adjectives printed in **bold** *type into nouns.*

1 **able**   He has the _____ to become a professional tennis player, but I'm not sure if he's dedicated enough.

2 **beautiful** This part of the country is well known as an area of great natural _____.

3 **boring**   We nearly died of _____ when we went to see the new opera. It was dreadful!

4 **distant**   Is the _____ from Earth to Mars the same as that from Earth to Venus?

5 **easy**   She was extremely intelligent and passed all her exams with _____.

6 **envious**   He was filled with _____ when he saw his neighbour's new car.

7 **famous**   The new pop group was so successful in Britain that their _____ soon spread to Europe and America.

8 **free**   The prisoner escaped to _____ by hiding in the boot of a visitor's car.

9 **friendly**   What started as _____ soon turned into love.

10 **grateful**   They couldn't show enough _____ when he saved their daughter from drowning.

11 **happy**   They say that money can't buy you _____, but I certainly wouldn't mind suffering in comfort.

12 **healthy**   'Your _____ would improve a lot if you lost some weight and exercised more,' the doctor told her.

13 **horrible**   People watched in _____ as the helicopter crashed into a nearby television mast.

14 **poor**   Freedom from _____ should be a human right.

15 **proud**   Although she was poor, her _____ wouldn't allow her to accept any form of charity.

16 **real**   He seemed friendly, but in _____ he was only after her money.

17 **short**   There is a great _____ of houses in most major cities.

18 **thirsty**   Give me something to drink please, mum. I'm dying of _____!

19 **true**   Is there any _____ in the rumour that the Prime Minister is going to resign?

20 **valuable**   It is very difficult to put a true _____ on this painting.

Changing verbs into nouns (various endings)

*Fill the gaps in each of the sentences below by changing the verbs
printed in **bold** type into nouns.*

1 **appear**   You should always take special care with your
_____ when you go for an interview.

2 **behave**   The children's _____ at the party was
dreadful.

3 **believe**   It is my _____ that a flying saucer will
land in a city on Earth before the year 2000.

4 **compare**   There is no _____ between his latest
book and his earlier ones.

5 **compete**   They say that _____ between companies
helps to keep prices down.

6 **decide**   Well, we can't stay here all day talking, can we?
We've got to make a _____ soon.

7 **depart**   Their _____ was delayed because of bad
weather.

8 **destroy**   The bombs caused terrible _____.

9 **entertain**   Holiday camps usually provide free
_____.

10 **inform**   I wrote off to the company asking for further
_____ about their offer.

11 **meet**   I'm afraid I can't come with you tonight, Pete. I've
got to go to a _____.

12 **paint**   This is a very early _____ by Turner.

13 **permit**   We had to get special _____ to leave
early.

14 **please**   Goodbye. It's been a _____ to meet you.

15 **prove**   I want _____ of your love. Lend me
£1,000!

16 **rob**   There was a _____ at the local post office
at the weekend.

17 **serve**   The _____ at the hotel was excellent.

18 **speak**   As best man, he had to make a _____ at the wedding.

19 **translate**   They've made a very good job on this _____. It's almost as good as the original.

20 **weigh**   If you want to lose _____, you'd better eat less.

Nouns from phrasal verbs

1 *Match the nouns from phrasal verbs (1–10) with their meanings (a–j). Write your answers in the boxes at the bottom of the page.*

1 breakdown

2 break-in

3 break-up

4 check-up

5 downpour

6 drawback

7 hold-up

8 output

9 write-off

10 write-up

a a heavy fall of rain

b the amount of something produced (e.g. goods at a factory)

c a written report of a play or new project; a review

d something which causes a delay (e.g. of traffic)

e the coming to an end of a relationship

f a sudden mechanical failure (e.g. a car engine)

g something which is so badly damaged in an accident that it is not worth repairing

h a medical examination to see if your health is all right

i a difficulty or disadvantage

j the entering of a building illegally and by force; a burglary

1	2	3	4	5	6	7	8	9	10

2 *Now complete the following dialogues with a suitable noun. Choose from the list on the previous page.*

1 A: Who won the tennis final?

   B: We don't know yet, they're still playing. There was a _____ earlier on so they stopped play for 90 minutes.

2 A: You don't usually walk, Paul. What's up?

   B: Haven't you heard? I had an accident last week and my car's a _____.

3 A: You're late again!

   B: I couldn't help it. I had a _____ on the motor-way.

4 A: Was the play good?

   B: Yes, we thought so. But it got a terrible _____ in today's papers. The critics hated it.

5 A: Do you like your new job?

   B: Yes, very much. The only _____ is that I have to spend so much time travelling.

6 A: Anne seems very unhappy these days.

   B: Yes, she hasn't been the same since the _____ of her marriage.

7 A: How many lawnmowers does the factory produce each week?

   B: I haven't got the exact figures, but I think the weekly _____ is about 500.

8 A: You look nervous, Frank.

   B: I am. I'm about to go to my doctor for a _____. I'm worried he's going to find something wrong with me.

9 A: There was another _____ last night – at number 10.

   B: Right, that's it! Tomorrow I'm getting a burglar alarm.

10 A: Excuse me, Has the train for Hastings left yet?

B: It hasn't come in yet, sir. There's been some sort of
_____ outside Tunbridge Wells. But it should
arrive soon.

Section Six: Adjectives, verbs and prepositions

Adjectives: Synonyms

Complete the table below with words that are similar in meaning to the ones given. Choose from the following:

attractive	enormous	glad	scared
boring	evil	impolite	silent
broad	expensive	incorrect	terrible
crazy	famous	marvellous	unhappy
eager	fast	peculiar	well-mannered

		Synonym				Synonym
1	awful			11	quiet	
2	dear (money)			12	rude	
3	dull			13	sad	
4	frightened			14	strange	
5	good-looking			15	very big	
6	happy			16	well-known	
7	keen			17	wicked	
8	mad			18	wide	
9	polite			19	wonderful	
10	quick			20	wrong	

Adjectives: Opposites

*Fill the gaps in the sentences below with adjectives that are opposite in meaning to the words printed in **bold** type. Choose from the following:*

absent	exciting	mean	shallow
alive	imaginary	noisy	single
amateur	lazy	odd	stale
asleep	loose	public	tame

1 Nothing seems to fit me these days! This dress is too **tight** and the other one's too _____.

2 The swimming pool is **deep** at this end but _____ at the other.

3 Most of today's _____ animals were once **wild**.

4 Peter Pan is an _____ character, I tell you! He isn't **real**.

5 I want the names of everyone who was **present** at the meeting and everyone who was _____.

6 It's nice to have a **quiet** weekend after a week of _____ parties.

7 He asked me if I was **married** or _____.

8 Is there a big difference between _____ and **professional** boxing?

9 Are Scottish people supposed to be **generous** or _____?

10 This is a **private** tennis court, but there are two _____ ones not far from here.

11 'Is Harold **awake**?'
   'No, he's _____.'
   'All right, I'll come back in an hour or two.'

12 This loaf is _____. I'd better go out and buy a **fresh** one.

13 I bought a Wild West poster the other day which said: 'WANTED: **DEAD** OR _____ JESSE JAMES'.

14 I hope tonight's film is _____ for a change. The last two we've seen have been so **boring**.

15 Houses with _____ numbers are on this side and those with **even** numbers are on the other.

16 Most of the students were very **hard-working**, but as usual there were one or two who were rather _____.

Useful adjectives 1

Complete each of the sentences below with a suitable adjective. Choose from the following:

busy	different	healthy	rusty
chilly	fashionable	juicy	secret
dangerous	favourite	noisy	serious
delicious	guilty	popular	valuable

1 He felt very _____ about putting his mother in an old-people's home instead of taking care of her himself.

2 She is the most _____ boss we've ever had. Very few people dislike her.

3 This vase is very _____. If I sold it I'd get at least £10,000 for it.

4 Although they were twins, they were very _____, both in looks and personality.

5 I can't come out tonight, I'm afraid. I'm far too _____. In fact, I've got so much to do at the moment that I probably won't be able to come out at all this week.

6 The party was so _____ that their neighbours phoned the police to complain.

7 The children had a _____ hiding-place which no one – not even their parents – knew about.

8 This fish is absolutely _____, Mary! You must give me the recipe.

9 We've decided to lead a _____ life from now on. So no more drinking or smoking for us, just lots of exercise, fresh air and proper food.

10 Put a jumper on, Pat. It's quite _____ out.

11 'How is she, doctor?'
'I'm afraid it's very _____, Mr James. We're going to have to operate immediately.'

12 What a _____ orange! Pass me a serviette, please. My hands are really sticky.

13 His parents wouldn't let him go hang-gliding. They thought it was too _____ and he might get killed.

14 'What's your _____ TV programme?'
'*Eastenders*, I think. Or the news.'

15 If you leave your bike out in the rain all the time it will get _____.

16 Wearing ties and waistcoats is very _____ again.

Useful adjectives 2

Complete each of the sentences below with a suitable adjective. Choose from the following:

average	excellent	regular	slippery
blind	natural	ripe	temporary
deaf	necessary	risky	useful
disappointing	practical	rotten	willing

1 'Is it _____ for both of us to sign to take money out of the account?'

'No, either you or your husband can do it.'

2 Be careful when you drive home tonight. The roads are very _____.

3 Would you be _____ to let my brother stay with you when he comes to London next weekend?

4 The _____ salary in this country is about £13,000 a year.

5 I don't care what you say, George, I still think it's _____ to want to get married and have children.

6 You'd better throw these bananas away – they're _____!

7 My father can't see. In fact, he's been _____ since he was 17.

8 Tom Browning is a very _____ person to know. He has lots of contacts and can probably find you work.

9 My wife and I are _____ theatregoers. We go at least once a month.

10 The film was very _____. We had expected it to be much better after all the publicity and everything.

11 Investing in stocks and shares is quite _____ compared to putting your money in a bank or a building society.

12 The job is just a _____ one until the end of August. Still, it's better than not having a job at all.

13 My cousin can't hear. She's _____.

14 Don't pick those apples – they're not _____ yet!

15 This work is _____. It's the best you've ever done. I'm really pleased with it.

16 We couldn't give him the job because he'd never done this sort of work before and we needed someone with lots of _____ experience.

Verbs: Synonyms

Complete the table below with words that are similar in meaning to the ones given. Choose from the following:

adore	brag	occur	scare
alter	depart	permit	speak
assist	detest	purchase	stumble
attempt	enter	repair	vanish
bathe	inquire	require	weep

		Synonym				Synonym
1	allow		11	happen	
2	ask		12	hate	
3	boast		13	help	
4	buy		14	leave	
5	change		15	love	
6	cry		16	mend	
7	disappear		17	need	
8	fall		18	swim	
9	frighten		19	talk	
10	go in		20	try	

Verbs: Opposites

*Fill the gaps in the sentences below with verbs that are opposite in meaning to the words printed in **bold** type. Choose from the following verbs and make any changes that may be necessary.*

admit	catch	destroy	save
allow	contract	lower	succeed
arrive	defend	mend	vanish
can't stand	demolish	reject	win

1 If they start a war now they are going to _____ everything they **have created** since they became independent.

2 We were surprised when he **failed** to get the contract as he usually _____ at everything he tried.

3 'I **adore** eating food with garlic in it.'
  'Do you? I don't. I _____ the smell!'

4 'Someone **has broken** my kite.'
  'Don't worry. I'll _____ it for you.'

5 Last season, Manchester United _____ eighteen matches and only **lost** three.

6 When you heat metal, it **expands**, and when it cools again it _____ .

7 'You stole the watch, didn't you? Come on, _____ it!'
  'No, I didn't. I **deny** everything.'

8 The government is talking about **raising** income tax and _____ VAT.

9 The man wrote off to his car insurance company saying: 'A car **appeared** from nowhere, hit my car, then _____ .'

10 We **depart** at 11.30 in the morning and _____ at midnight.

11 In a recession, people tend to _____ money rather than **spend** it.

12 If a country is **attacked**, then it has the right and the duty to _____ itself.

13 'Here, _____ this!'
'No, don't throw it! I'll only **drop** it.'

14 At first she **accepted** our ideas, but in the end she _____ them.

15 They are going to _____ the old cinema to **build** a new supermarket.

16 'I won't _____ you to stay out all night. I absolutely **forbid** it!' said the father to his 13-year-old daughter.

Useful verbs 1

*Match up the verbs (1–16) on the left with a suitable phrase (a–p)
from the list on the right. Write your answers in the boxes at the
bottom of the page.*

1	apply for	a	a new planet
2	beat	b	your finger with a hammer
3	borrow	c	someone money
4	discover	d	someone at tennis
5	dive	e	tomatoes in the greenhouse
6	dry	f	in bed until 10.30
7	fasten	g	into the swimming pool
8	grow	h	the word correctly
9	hire	i	a new job in Canada
10	hit	j	the meeting because of illness
11	hurry	k	your seatbelt before the plane takes off
12	lie	l	for love
13	marry	m	£20 from someone
14	owe	n	yourself with a towel
15	postpone	o	a car for the weekend
16	pronounce	p	to catch the last bus home

1	2	3	4	5	6	7	8	9	10	11	12	13	14	15	16

Useful verbs 2

Match the verbs (1–16) on the left with a suitable phrase (a–p) from the list on the right. Write your answers in the boxes at the bottom of the page.

1 escape   a the child for being naughty

2 invite   b the book into Russian

3 offer   c over 75 kilos

4 practise   d from the cold

5 punish   e from prison

6 renew   f after a meal

7 return   g someone £2,000 for their car

8 shiver   h goodbye to your friends at the station

9 solve   i from holiday with a suntan

10 spend   j a suitcase

11 taste   k all your friends for dinner

12 translate   l the weekend in Paris

13 unpack   m the piano for two hours a day

14 wash up   n a difficult problem

15 wave   o your passport before you go abroad

16 weigh   p the soup to see if it needs more salt

1	2	3	4	5	6	7	8	9	10	11	12	13	14	15	16

Useful verbs 3

Complete the sentences below with a suitable verb. Choose from the following list and make any changes that may be necessary.

afford	end	obey	smile
apologize	fit	refuse	understand
arrange	fix	repeat	visit
cause	hurt	scream	waste
decide	lock	shine	worry

1 Don't forget to _____ the back door before you go to bed.

2 It was a beautiful day. The sun _____, there was no wind and the sky was blue.

3 Don't _____ your time talking to him – he's not going to change his mind.

4 Take your time; think it over carefully. You don't have to _____ this minute. You can let me know on Monday.

5 'There's a broken window in the greenhouse.'
'Don't worry. I'll _____ it.'

6 I'm sorry, I didn't hear what you said. Could you _____ it, please?

7 I don't speak any foreign languages apart from French, so when I visited Russia last summer I couldn't _____ a word people said.

8 I'd like to buy a new car, but I can't _____ it at the moment.

9 'Do you know what time the film _____?'
'At 10.30, I think.'

10 She was so frightened by the sudden noise that she _____.

11 Most parents _____ if their children are out late at night. It's only natural.

12 He _____ for arriving late at the meeting.

13 If you hit your thumb with a hammer, it _____.

14 Now I want this to be a happy photograph, so _____ everyone!

15 These shoes don't _____ – they're too small.

16 We usually _____ my parents at the weekend. (My mother likes to cook Sunday lunch for us.)

17 Would you like me to _____ a meeting between you and Ms Sayers?

18 Soldiers are trained to _____ orders without question.

19 Most people know nowadays that smoking can _____ lung cancer.

20 I asked her to help us, but she _____.

Useful verbs 4

Complete the sentences below with a suitable verb. Choose from the following list and make any changes that may be necessary.

admire	blame	fetch	pretend
annoy	contain	follow	produce
avoid	continue	hide	remind
behave	demand	multiply	rush
belong to	doubt	point	trust

1 He marched angrily into the shop and in a loud voice _____ to see the manager.

2 'What do you get if you _____ 15 by 25?'
'375, I think.'

3 _____ me to phone my mother tonight, will you? She'll kill me if I forget.

4 Do you know who this scarf _____? I found it under the chair.

5 Could you go upstairs, Frank, and _____ my slippers, please?

6 I wouldn't _____ him, if I were you. He's very dishonest.

7 The only politician my father ever really _____ was John F. Kennedy.

8 I think my cat thinks it's a dog. It _____ me everywhere.

9 We'll have to _____ if we're going to catch the last bus home. It leaves in two minutes.

10 I wish he wouldn't eat with his mouth open. It really _____ me.

11 He didn't want to be seen, so he _____ behind the sofa.

12 'Can you tell me what this packet _____, sir?' the customs officer asked the man.

13 'Do you know what they _____ at the factory over there?'
'Washing machines, I think.'

14 Would you like to stop now or shall we _____ for a while longer?

15 He may pass his driving test, but I _____ it. He's too nervous.

16 Take the top road if you want to _____ the rush hour traffic.

17 I said hello to her but she _____ not to notice me.

18 'It's not my fault! Don't _____ me. I didn't do it,' the girl said to her mother.

19 'Now try to _____ yourselves,' the mother said, as she dropped her children off at the party.

20 The policeman asked her to look at the five men in the line-up and to _____ to anyone she recognized.

Verbs that usually follow certain nouns

Which verbs usually go after the nouns (1–16) on the left? Choose from the ones (a–p) on the right. Some verbs can be used with more than one noun, but try to use each once only. Write your answers in the boxes at the bottom of the page.

1	a river	a	boils
2	a plane	b	breaks
3	memories	c	breaks out
4	a strike	d	burns
5	a fire	e	explodes
6	ice	f	fade
7	a kettle	g	falls
8	an alarm clock	h	flies
9	darkness	i	flows
10	a bomb	j	goes off
11	the sun	k	happens
12	day	l	is called
13	a doorbell	m	lands
14	an accident	n	melts in the sun
15	war	o	rings
16	time	p	rises in the east

1	2	3	4	5	6	7	8	9	10	11	12	13	14	15	16

Verbs to do with movement

Write the missing verbs in the sentences below. Choose from the following list and make any changes that may be necessary.

bend down	dash	march	stagger
chase	hop	pick up	stand
climb	jump	ride	stroll
cycle	limp	slide	throw

1 Kangaroos don't really run, they _____.
2 They _____ along the cliff path, admiring the view of the English Channel.
3 'Stop thief!' she shouted as she _____ the thief through the park.
4 'Do you _____?'
  'Oh yes. In fact I've got my own horse.'
5 She dropped her pen, so she _____ to pick it up.
6 The children kicked the ball into his garden and asked him to _____ it back to them.
7 From a very early age it had always been her ambition to _____ Mount Everest.
8 We had to _____ across the stream as there wasn't a footbridge.
9 The drunken man _____ home along the pavement.
10 After getting a mountain bike as a birthday present he decided to _____ to work instead of using the car.
11 There were no seats left in the hall by the time we got there, so we had to _____ at the back.
12 He _____ across the street to catch a bus on the other side.
13 There was ice on the pavement and the children were having great fun _____ down it.

14 The soldiers _____ proudly through the streets to celebrate the Queen's 80th birthday.

15 He was _____ so badly after being kicked on the ankle that he was forced to leave the pitch and a substitute came on.

16 'Don't leave your clothes all over the floor,' the mother said to her 10-year-old daughter. '_____ them _____!'

Verbs to do with speaking and looking

Write the missing verbs in the sentences below. Choose from the following list and make any changes that may be necessary.

announce	gaze	notice	stutter
catch someone's	glance	peep	swear
eye	gossip	peer	whisper
confess	grumble	stare	yell
examine			

1 You were miles away this morning, Paul. You walked right past me without even _____ me.

2 'W-w-when's the n-n-next b-b-bus, please?' he _____.

3 The two lovers _____ into each other's eyes, completely oblivious to the rest of the world.

4 'It's always me, I'm the one who always has to do the washing-up,' he _____. 'Why can't Jenny do it for a change?'

5 British Rail _____ that the 12.30 train from Brighton had been delayed and was now running twenty minutes late.

6 'Pass the ball! Pass it!' the football coach _____ in a loud voice.

7 He _____ at me intently without blinking. In the end I had to look away.

8 Don't tell Billy anything about your private life or the whole village will know about it. He _____ a lot.

9 'I love you,' he _____ quietly to his wife, so that none of the other passengers could hear.

10 She wanted to pay the bill, so she tried to _____ the waiter's _____.

11 There was no answer, so she _____ through the letterbox to see if anyone was at home.

12 She picked up the radio, _____ it carefully, then put it down again.

13 He _____ loudly when he missed the nail and hit his thumb with the hammer instead.

14 After seven hours of being questioned by the police, he finally _____. 'All right, all right, I stole the money!' he said.

15 He _____ at the clock on the office wall again to see if it was lunchtime, saw there was still five minutes to go, so carried on working.

16 He _____ through the mist trying to read the signpost.

Prepositions with nouns

Write the missing prepositions in the sentences below. You can use each preposition more than once. Choose from the following:

at	by	for	in	on

1 We are related _____ marriage. He is my wife's brother.

2 After taking his driving test seven times, _____ the end he passed.

3 I'm afraid Ms Collins is in Germany _____ business this week. Can I help instead?

4 I didn't really like him _____ first, but now we are really good friends.

5 They travelled to Italy _____ air.

6 'Could I speak to Ruby, please?'
'She's not here _____ the moment. Can I take a message?'

7 Things have changed a lot in this country. _____ example, most families have cars nowadays.

8 There must be something wrong with Thomas. He hasn't been _____ love for at least three weeks.

9 No chips for me, please. I'm _____ a diet.

10 There was a large sign outside the house which said '_____ SALE'.

Prepositions with adjectives

Write the missing prepositions in the sentences below. You can use each preposition more than once. Choose from the following.:

at	for	in	of	to	with

1 My wife is addicted _____ cigarettes. She just can't give them up.

2 This season he has been successful _____ every golf tournament he has entered.

3 She was very angry _____ her boss for making them work overtime.

4 He was never very good _____ sport when he was at school, so we were really surprised when we heard he had become a professional footballer.

5 You ought to be ashamed _____ yourself. How could you speak to your parents like that?

6 She was very grateful _____ him for all his help.

7 We all felt very sorry _____ her after first her husband then her eldest son were killed.

8 'The match has been cancelled.'

'Are you sure _____ that?'

'Yes. Brian phoned me to tell me.'

9 When we looked out of the window in the morning we found that the lawn was covered _____ snow.

10 She got the job because she was experienced _____ book-keeping.

11 How could you do it, Paulina? I'm surprised _____ you!

12 He has been ill _____ flu for over a week.

13 My husband is very fond _____ sweets – and it shows! He's twice as fat now as he was when we got married.

14 Can you think of a suitable present _____ a 6-year-old boy?

15 This type of jacket is very popular _____ teenagers.

16 They had a large, detached house close _____ the beach.

17 The room was full _____ boxes and old furniture.

18 Who is responsible _____ locking up the shop at night?

19 I'm sorry, I'll have to go out of the room I'm afraid. I'm allergic _____ cats.

20 My flat is right in the centre of town, which is very convenient _____ the office.

Prepositions with verbs

Write the missing prepositions in the sentences below. You can use each preposition more than once. Choose from the following:

at	from	on
about	in	to
for	of	with

1 The train to Manchester departs _____ platform 12.

2 His grandmother died _____ cancer at the age of 92.

3 He ended his concert _____ his big number one hit 'Love you only'.

4 Most parents hope _____ a better life for their children.

5 The children laughed _____ the clown when he fell into a big bucket of water.

6 She lives _____ Grove Road, next to the post office.

7 I prefer tea _____ coffee.

8 'Doesn't the new boss remind you _____ Mel Gibson?' 'No, not a bit. I think you need glasses!'

9 I see the company's advertising _____ a new manager. Why don't you apply?

10 I see Janet has quarrelled _____ her mother again.

11 Which horse shall we bet _____ in the next race?

12 'Did you bring the book I asked you for?' 'Oh, sorry! I forgot all _____ it!'

13 This book has been translated _____ French into English.

14 I find it very difficult to concentrate _____ my work when it's such a lovely day outside.

15 She apologized _____ arriving late.

16 'Don't forget to write _____ me at least once a week,' her fiancé said as he said goodbye to her at the airport.

17 'Why are you crying? What's happened?'
   'It's Brian. He threw a stone _____ me!'
18 Do you believe _____ God?
19 There was a large sign on the gate which said 'BEWARE _____ THE DOG'.
20 She's always worrying _____ her health. That's what's made her ill, if you ask me.

Three-part phrasal verbs

1 *Match the three-part phrasal verbs (1–10) with their meanings (a–j). Write your answers in the boxes at the bottom of the page..*

1 drop in on

2 drop out of

3 face up to

4 get around/round to

5 get along/on with

6 hang on to

7 look back on

8 look out for

9 make up for

10 stand in for

a be on friendly terms with someone

b remember, think about the past

c keep something instead of selling it or giving it away

d take someone's place or job for a short time

e accept something (e.g. an unpleasant fact)

f pay someone a short, casual visit

g manage to find time to do something (often after a long delay)

h compensate for

i withdraw from something (e.g. a race)

j watch for something or somebody

1	2	3	4	5	6	7	8	9	10

2 *Now complete the following dialogues with a suitable phrasal verb. Choose from the above list.*

1 A: How's James after the operation?

  B: Not too good, I'm afraid. He still refuses to _____ the fact that he'll never walk again.

2 A: If I were you, Patrick, I'd _____ this vase.

  B: Why? It's ugly!

  A: Maybe. But it's worth a lot of money. It's Chinese.

3 A: Anne's being very nice today.

  B: I know. She's probably trying to _____ all the trouble she caused yesterday.

4 A: I'm going to Brighton next week. That's where your sister lives, isn't it?

  B: That's right. Why don't you _____ her? She'd love to see you again.

5 A: You look excited, Tom.

  B: I am. The leading actor's ill, so they've asked me to _____ him tonight. It might be my big chance!

6 A: I often _____ the 'sixties and think what great times we had then.

  B: Yes, those were the days, all right.

7 A: Did Pam Baker win last Saturday's race?

  B: No, she had to _____ it, after falling and twisting her ankle.

8 A: How's the new flat?

  B: It's fine. I love it. But I'm finding it a bit hard to_____ my new neighbours. They've got young children and don't like me playing music after nine o'clock.

9 A: Have you written to Claire yet?

  B: I keep meaning to, but I just can't seem to _____ it. I'm just too busy at the moment.

10 A: We're off to the Grand National next weekend.

  B: Well, _____ pickpockets!

Check 2

This is a check to see how many words you can remember from Section Four, Section Five and Section Six. Try to do it without looking back at the previous pages.

1 Which of the following is usually found in the classroom?

   (a) subjects   (b) wall chart   (c) caption   (d) horoscope

2 She hated school, so she often _____.

   (a) played truant   (b) expelled   (c) failed   (d) broke out

3 What's this?

   (a) a pencil sharpener

   (b) a set square

   (c) a ruler

   (d) a protractor

4 Which of the following is not a state school?

   (a) a primary school   (b) a prep school

   (c) a comprehensive school   (d) a Sixth-Form College

5 She's in her first year at university. She's _____.

   (a) a pupil   (b) an apprentice   (c) a scholar   (d) an undergraduate

6 What does a teacher fill in to show that a pupil is present or absent in class?

   (a) an exercise book   (b) a register   (c) a timetable   (d) a footnote

7 Which part of a book is this?

   (a) the jacket

   (b) the cover

   (c) the title

   (d) the appendix

8 Which of the following books is fiction?

   (a) a biography   (b) a manual   (c) a directory   (d) a thriller

150

9 In which of the following TV programmes does someone talk to a number of famous guests?

(a) a soap opera (b) a documentary (c) a chat show

(d) a quiz show

10 Which of the following parts of a newspaper would you read to know more about the private lives of famous people?

(a) the colour supplement   (b) the editorial

(c) the gossip column   (d) the comic strip

11 In each of the following groups of four words, one does not fit in. <u>Underline</u> the word and try to say why it is different from the rest.

(a) cupboard, shelf, bookcase, calculator

(b) Polytechnic, Teacher Training College, secondary school, College of Further Education

(c) caretaker, vice-chancellor, principal, headteacher

(d) atlas, cookery book, whodunnit, dictionary

(e) column, chapter, circulation, article

12 There are fifteen words hidden in the following word square.
They are all words to do with education. See how many you can
find. You can read vertically (*5 words*), horizontally (*5 words*) or
diagonally (*5 words*).

```
S   T   A   F   F   H   A   D   R   C   K   U   M   I   T   F
C   T   E   X   T   B   O   O   K   D   O   F   O   P   B   U
M   C   O   B   E   H   G   A   S   T   G   U   J   L   I   N
I   R   K   E   Y   R   R   E   N   O   T   I   R   I   C   I
T   O   W   S   T   L   A   P   P   B   D   M   I   S   H   V
V   U   J   U   B   I   D   P   A   U   A   N   G   A   E   E
A   C   T   E   R   H   U   S   U   R   S   H   E   T   S   R
C   R   O   O   F   D   A   P   I   P   S   E   S   C   E   S
A   L   L   Q   R   A   T   I   N   M   I   S   S   H   Y   I
T   E   K   L   I   N   E   D   S   O   G   L   B   E   G   T
I   V   E   F   O   T   B   A   K   O   N   I   R   L   O   Y
O   S   H   O   M   E   W   O   R   K   M   A   N   Y   F   O
N   T   I   C   H   U   X   A   L   I   E   D   W   A   H   G
R   E   V   I   S   E   B   A   G   R   N   K   E   N   I   L
W   K   A   N   P   J   I   M   M   S   T   A   D   S   E   R
C   H   D   E   T   E   N   T   I   O   N   Q   S   T   K   G
```

13 Read the following sentences and try to work out what the
missing words are. To help you, the first and last letters of the
words are given.

(a) You use it to clean a board with. It's a d——r.

(b) I must e——l for a German course next term.

(c) When the headteacher is away, the d——y h——d takes over.

(d) The book is very popular and has sold lots of copies. It's a
b——t s——r.

(e) A book is often divided into a number of c———s.

(f) *The Sun* has the largest c————n of any British daily newspaper.

(g) After he died, his o————y appeared in *The Times*.

(h) She steals and lies a lot. She's very d————t.

(i) What a c————e chair!

(j) He lost his job in June and has been u————d ever since.

14 Match the words on the left with the ones on the right. Draw lines between the correct pairs.

attend	a driving test
behave	a poem
learn a poem	for her excellent work
leave school	in foreign languages
pass	a course
praise her	for an exam
punish her	by heart
recite	badly at the party
study	for not doing her homework
specialize	at the age of 17

15 Say whether the following sentences are correct (C) or incorrect (I)?

(a) You use an **overhead projector** to see distant objects clearly.

(b) Another word for **satchel** is **schoolbag**.

(c) You go to **playschool** before the age of five.

(d) **Fiction** involves real characters and events.

(e) A **preface** is very similar to a **foreword**.

(f) You have to do it – it's **compulsory**.

(g) A **tabloid** newspaper is larger than a normal-sized newspaper.

(h) She's fainted. Throw some water on her face to make her **come round**.

(i) There was a **break-up** last night at the flat next to mine. Fortunately, nothing much was stolen.

(j) She can't see. She's **deaf**.

16 Fill the gaps in the sentences below by changing the words printed in **bold** type into nouns.

(a) **arrive**   Their _____ was delayed for two hours because of the bad weather.

(b) **insure**   Running a car is very expensive. Apart from the petrol costs and road tax, there is also _____.

(c) **describe**   For homework, we had to write a _____ of someone we knew well.

(d) **invent**   If it wasn't for the _____ of television, I don't know what we'd do in the evenings.

(e) **disappoint** It was always a great _____ to him that his parents weren't millionaires.

(f) **weak**   My brother never cries. He regards crying and showing your feelings as a sign of _____.

(g) **deep**   Do you know what the _____ of the river is at this point?

(h) **know**   Although she had only been studying the subject for just over a year, her _____ about it impressed us all.

(i) **boring**   My cousin's idea of _____ is to listen to opera all day.

(j) **poor**   I am always shocked to find that there are still people in Britain who live in great _____.

(k) **famous**   Cathy won't even say hello to her old friends
                    now. Since winning that gold medal at the
                    last Olympic Games, _____ has
                    really gone to her head.

(l) **appear**   We didn't recognize him at first because his
                    _____ had changed such a lot.

(m)**compete**   My mother won a newspaper
                    _____ last week, where the first
                    prize was a weekend for two in Paris.

(n) **permit**   Because he was a foreigner, he had to have
                    special _____ to buy a house in
                    this country.

(o) **speak**   'What did you think of Clive's _____?'
                    'Boring as usual.'

17 Complete the following sentences. To help you, the first letter
of the answer is given.

(a) A synonym for **dull** is b_____.

(b) A synonym for **wide** is b_____.

(c) A synonym for **expensive** is d_____.

(d) A synonym for **very big** is e_____.

(e) A synonym for **strange** is p_____.

(f) A synonym for **to cry** is to w_____.

(g) A synonym for **to disappear** is to v_____.

(h) A synonym for **to try** is to a_____.

(i) A synonym for **to go in** is to e_____.

(j) A synonym for **to frighten** is to s_____.

18 Complete the following sentences. To help you, the first letter of the answer is given.

    (a) The opposite of **present** is a_____.

    (b) The opposite of **hard-working** is l_____.

    (c) The opposite of **real** is i_____.

    (d) The opposite of **deep** is s_____.

    (e) The opposite of **fresh** bread is s_____ bread.

    (f) The opposite of **to deny** is to a_____.

    (g) The opposite of **to refuse** is to a_____.

    (h) The opposite of **to attack** is to d_____.

    (i) The opposite of **to create** is to d_____.

    (j) The opposite of **to spend** money is to s_____ money.

19 Supply the missing prepositions in the following sentences.

    (a) She went to Japan last month _____ business.

    (b) Do you think I should go _____ a diet, Jenny?

    (c) He was very angry _____ us for not letting him know that we would be late.

    (d) Most children are fond _____ sweets.

    (e) She was good _____ all sports.

    (f) Leave everything to Ken. He is very experienced _____ dealing with the police.

    (g) Excuse me, which terminal do flights for Copenhagen depart _____?

    (h) He died _____ a heart attack at the age of 46.

    (i) Let us now end _____ that well-known song 'We shall overcome'.

    (j) My cousin translated this poem _____ Finnish into English.

20 Complete the following dialogues with a suitable phrasal verb. The words in brackets after each dialogue should help you. In (d) and (e), a noun made from a phrasal verb is needed.

(a) A: Your daughter is very good at sport, isn't she?

B: Yes, she _____ her father. He once played rugby for Scotland. *(is like)*

(b) A: Do you speak German?

B: Yes, I _____ it _____ when I taught there a few years ago. *(learnt to speak it)*

(c) A: That's the last time I ever speak to him!

B: Don't tell me – you and Brian have _____ again. *(quarrelled)*

(d) A: Tom's late again!

B: Yes, and I bet he uses the same excuse about his car having a _____ on the way here. *(his car stopping working)*

(e) A: What a _____! *(heavy shower of rain)*

B: Yes, I thought the rain would never stop.

(f) A: If you're ever in Brighton, do _____ us. *(pay us a visit)*

B: Thank you. I'd love to.

(g) A: Do you _____ your mother-in-law? *(have a good relationship with)*

B: Yes, we're very good friends.

(h) A: You want to _____ that painting. It's worth a lot of money. *(keep, not sell)*

B: Really? I thought it was rubbish.

(i) A: Good morning. I'm David Smith. I shall be _____ Mr Wilkins this week. *(taking the place of, deputising for)*

B: How do you do. Pleased to meet you.

(j) A: I must be getting old. I keep _____ the old days and thinking how great they were. *(recalling, remembering)*

B: Don't worry, I do the same.

21 Here are thirty words in alphabetical order. Place each word under the correct heading (*5 words under each*).

academic	classified ads	memoirs
acknowledgements	contents	pencil
anthology	encyclopedia	review
article	expert	romantic novel
autobiography	felt-tip pen	seminar
ballpoint pen	governor	sports page
bibliography	graduate	student
biro	headline	term
blurb	index	tutor
chalk	lecture	tutorial

Things you write with

_____

_____

_____

_____

_____

People in education

_____

_____

_____

_____

_____

Other words to do with education

_____

_____

_____

_____

_____

Types of books

_____

_____

_____

_____

_____

Parts of a book

_____

_____

_____

_____

_____

Parts of a newspaper

_____

_____

_____

_____

_____

Answers

Section One: People

Types of people 1 (pages 3 and 4)

1	optimist	6	tourist	11	colleague	16	employee
2	spectator	7	bachelor	12	motorist	17	racist
3	widow	8	pedestrian	13	pessimist	18	neighbour
4	boyfriend	9	employer	14	spinster	19	lodger
5	partner	10	vegetarian	15	fiancée	20	acquaintance

Types of people 2 (pages 4 and 5)

1	landlord	6	boss	11	client	16	victim
2	refugee	7	heir	12	twin	17	opponent
3	predecessor	8	ancestor	13	invalid	18	gossip
4	celebrity	9	patient	14	survivor	19	orphan
5	customer	10	successor	15	rival	20	tenant

Describing people: Physical appearance

1 (pages 6 and 7)

Age	Height	Hair	Other words
in his/her early twenties	above average height	dark-haired	attractive
in his/her mid thirties	below average height	fair-haired	dark-skinned
in his/her mid to late sixties	quite tall	going bald	good-looking
just turned fifty	**Figure/build**	has a beard (*or under* Other words)	handsome
quite old	muscular	has a moustache (*or under* Other words)	has a beard (*or under* Hair)
quite young	of medium build	shoulder length	has a moustache (*or under* Hair)
	plump	straight	pretty
	skinny	swept back	tanned
		thick, black	
		with a fringe	
		with a parting	

2 (page 9)

Number 2.

Describing people: Character and personality 1 (pages 12 and 13)

1	clever	6	greedy	11	materialistic	16	bossy
2	honest	7	optimistic	12	pessimistic	17	easy-going
3	modest	8	bad-tempered	13	big-headed	18	impulsive
4	affectionate	9	cheerful	14	forgetful	19	childish
5	cruel	10	friendly	15	lively	20	brave

Describing people: Character and personality 2 (pages 14 and 15)

1	self-confident	6	arrogant	11	vain	16	proud
2	cowardly	7	witty	12	self-conscious	17	dishonest
3	sensitive	8	stubborn	13	well-behaved	18	sympathetic
4	talkative	9	selfish	14	cautious	19	strict
5	punctual	10	kind	15	reliable	20	frank

Follow up (page 15)

Free choice

Describing people: Moods and feelings 1 (pages 16 and 17)

1	lonely	5	embarrassed	9	sleepy	13	excited
2	guilty	6	nervous	10	bored	14	ashamed
3	relieved	7	angry	11	bitter	15	curious
4	afraid	8	disappointed	12	depressed		

Describing people: Moods and feelings 2 (pages 17 and 18)

1	hurt	5	upset	9	tense	13	in a bad mood
2	restless	6	confused	10	proud	14	helpless
3	exhausted	7	in a good mood	11	shocked	15	frustrated
4	giddy	8	disgusted	12	envious		

Follow up (page 19) *Suggestions only. Other answers may be possible.*

1	nervous	4	envious	7	afraid	9	disappointed
2	lonely	5	embarrassed	8	relieved	10	angry
3	excited	6	shocked				

Jobs

1 (pages 20 and 21)

1	fireman	6	baker	11	secretary	16	cleaner
2	teacher	7	plumber	12	bricklayer	17	hairdresser
3	mechanic	8	nurse	13	photographer	18	lorry driver
4	dentist	9	traffic warden	14	butcher		
5	postman	10	dustman	15	doctor		

2 (pages 22 and 23)

1	– h	5	– p	9	– i	13	– b
2	– e	6	– n	10	– o	14	– j
3	– l	7	– k	11	– f	15	– g
4	– c	8	– a	12	– m	16	– d

Who's in charge? (page 24)

1	– e	5	– i	9	– f	13	– j
2	– h	6	– a	10	– b	14	– l
3	– m	7	– d	11	– n	15	– c
4	– k	8	– o	12	– g		

Verbs to describe common bodily actions (pages 25 and 26)

1	crawl	6	licked	11	cry	16	blow your nose
2	smile	7	yawning	12	smell	17	nodded
3	whistle	8	laughing	13	winked	18	cough
4	kiss	9	chew	14	frowned	19	sneezing
5	blink	10	touch	15	lie down	20	breathe

Phrasal verbs

1 (page 27)

1	– c	4	– j	7	– i	9	– b
2	– h	5	– g	8	– e	10	– d
3	– f	6	– a				

2 (page 28)

1	go with	4	put off	7	gone out	9	get on
2	turn up	5	clear up	8	carry on	10	Hang on
3	broke down	6	takes off				

Section Two: Towns, travel and transport

In the town

1 (page 29)

6	advertisement	8	lamp-post	9	pavement	15	road sign
16	bridge	18	litter bin	11	pedestrian	25	subway
7	building site	24	multi-storey car		crossing	20	taxi rank
5	bus stop		park	23	pedestrian	4	telephone box
21	café	22	newspaper		precinct	19	tower block
2	department		vendor	17	pillar box	13	traffic island
	store	1	park	3	public	14	traffic lights
10	kerb	12	parking meter		conveniences		

2 (pages 29, and 30)

1	advertisement	5	department	7	pillar box	9	traffic island
2	traffic lights		store	8	public	10	subway
3	parking meter	6	pedestrian		conveniences		
4	litter bin		crossing				

161

Travelling by road

1 (page 32 and 33)

14	by-pass	17	diversion	19	junction	8	outside lane
5	central	9	flyover	13	lay-by	16	roundabout
	reservation	3	grass verge	18	level crossing	10	service area
4	crash barrier	11	hard shoulder	7	middle lane	2	slip road
20	crossroads	6	inside lane	1	motorway	12	underpass
15	cycle path						

2 (pages 32)

1	slip road	4	diversion	7	underpass	9	junction
2	lay-by	5	grass verge	8	level crossing	10	hard shoulder
3	bypass	6	outside lane				

Vehicles: Road transport (page 34)

2	ambulance	11	fire engine	8	motorbike	14	scooter
6	bicycle	15	hatchback	5	pick-up truck	1	sports car
10	bus	3	juggernaut	13	police car	4	taxi
16	coach	12	lorry	7	saloon car	9	van

Vehicles: Other forms of transport (page 35)

7	barge	10	horse and cart	12	liner	14	speedboat
11	canoe	1	hot-air balloon	2	motor boat	16	train
4	car ferry	8	hovercraft	13	plane	3	tram
15	dinghy	5	lifeboat	6	rowing boat	9	yacht

Parts of a car

Exterior (page 36)

9	aerial	2	headlight	20	rear light	4	windscreen
1	bonnet	11	indicator	18	rear window	5	windscreen
19	boot	13	lock	6	roof rack		wiper
3	bumper	10	number plate	15	tyre	7	wing
12	door handle	17	petrol cap	14	wheel	8	wing mirror
16	exhaust pipe						

Interior (page 37)

13	accelerator	3	dashboard	4	heater	1	rear-view
12	brake pedal,	19	driver's seat	7	horn		mirror
	foot brake	14	gear lever	17	ignition	20	seat-belt
16	car radio	2	glove	10	indicator switch	6	speedometer
5	choke		compartment	18	passenger seat	9	steering wheel
11	clutch	15	handbrake	8	petrol gauge		

Verbs to do with driving (pages 38 and 39)

1	keeps to the speed limit	5	accelerate	9	change gear	12	give way
2	reverse	6	overtake	10	does a U-turn	13	stalls
3	brake	7	tows	11	breaking the speed limit	14	broke down
4	dip your headlights	8	park			15	skid

Road signs (pages 39 and 40)

1	No right turn	5	Road works	9	No through road	13	Maximum speed
2	School crossing patrol	6	Uneven road	10	One way street	14	No parking
3	Bend to right	7	Airport	11	Level crossing ahead	15	No stopping
4	No entry	8	End of motorway	12	No overtaking		

Travelling by train (pages 41 and 42)

1	left-luggage office	8	platform	13	compartments	20	ticket collector
2	ticket office	9	trolley	14	platform	21	tickets
3	return	10	departures board	15	carriage	22	through train
4	timetable	11	platform	16	luggage rack	23	change
5	train	12	inter-city express	17	window seat	24	buffet car
6	platform			18	no smoking	25	restaurant car
7	catch			19	railway station		

Travelling by plane (pages 43 and 44)

1	long-term car park	8	non smoking	15	passport	20	Gate
2	Terminal	9	Aisle	16	immigration officer	21	took off
3	airport	10	Aisle	17	duty free	22	landed
4	check-in desk	11	boarding pass	18	departures board	23	baggage reclaim
5	check in (v)	12	flight	19	boarding	24	passport control
6	hand luggage	13	departure lounge			25	conveyor belt
7	airline ticket	14	security check			26	Customs

Phrasal verbs

1 (page 45)

1	– e	4	– j	7	– c	9	– b
2	– i	5	– a	8	– f	10	– g
3	– d	6	– h				

2 (page 46)

1	Look (it) up	4	call (it) off	7	call for	10	put (you) through
2	fill in	5	puts up with	8	turn (it) down		
3	set off	6	give (it) back	9	get in		

Section Three: Holidays and entertainment

Places to stay on holiday (pages 47 and 48)

1 campsite	4 hotel	7 holiday camp	9 youth hostel
2 spa	5 boarding house	... chalet	10 self-catering
3 bed and breakfast	6 caravan	8 motel	
... guest house			

Booking a holiday (page 49)

The correct order is:
6 – 10 – 15 – 1 – 8 – 13 – 3 – 11 – 2 – 12 – 5 – 9 – 14 – 7 – 4

Things you can do on holiday (page 50)

1 – h	5 – n	9 – m	12 – g
2 – l	6 – a	10 – f	13 – k
3 – e	7 – i	11 – b	14 – d
4 – j	8 – c		

Extracts from holiday brochures (pages 51 and 52)

1 destinations	8 restaurants	14 palm	20 Asia
2 Mediterranean	9 dishes	15 trip	21 unspoilt
3 scenery	10 coast	16 holiday-makers	22 breathtaking
4 mountains	11 sunshine	17 scuba diving	23 bays
5 beaches	12 spectacular	18 cuisine	24 markets
6 capital	13 Explore	19 picturesque	25 Sightseeing
7 villages			

Other useful holiday words (pages 53 and 54)

1 package tour	5 resort	9 excursion	12 itinerary
2 sunbathing	6 view ... balcony	10 visa	13 guidebook
3 brochures	7 phrase-book	11 beauty spot	14 cruise
4 foreign currency	8 holiday-makers		

At the seaside (pages 54 and 55)

11 beach	17 deck-chair	20 lifeguard	7 sea
12 beach hut	10 harbour	4 lighthouse	2 sea wall
18 beach-ball	6 horizon	5 pier	15 spade
14 bucket	1 hotel	19 sand	9 swimmer
3 cliff	13 kite	16 sandcastle	8 wave

Countries, nationalities and languages (page 56)

Country	Nationality	Language
Australia	Australian	English
Austria	Austrian	German
Belgium	Belgian	French, Flemish
Brazil	Brazilian	Portuguese
Britain	British	English, Welsh, Gaelic
Canada	Canadian	English, French
China	Chinese	Chinese
Denmark	Danish	Danish
Finland	Finnish	Finnish
France	French	French
Germany	German	German
Greece	Greek	Greek
Hungary	Hungarian	Hungarian
Italy	Italian	Italian
Japan	Japanese	Japanese
Norway	Norwegian	Norwegian
Poland	Polish	Polish
Portugal	Portuguese	Portuguese
Russia	Russian	Russian
Spain	Spanish	Spanish
Switzerland	Swiss	French, German, Italian
Turkey	Turkish	Turkish

Public holidays and special occasions (page 57)

1 – e 3 – b 5 – c 7 – d
2 – h 4 – g 6 – a 8 – f

The world of music: Musical Instruments (pages 58 and 59)

23	accordion	16	cymbal	18	kettledrum	15	triangle
22	bagpipes	4	double bass	13	oboe	7	trombone
21	banjo	11	flute	25	organ	6	trumpet
14	bassoon	8	French horn	24	piano	9	tuba
19	bongoes	20	harmonica	10	saxophone	2	viola
3	cello	5	harp	17	tambourine	1	violin
12	clarinet						

The world of music: A pop group (pages 60 and 61)

1	keyboard player	5	amplifier	9	drum kit	13	guitarists
2	electric piano	6	lead singer	10	backing group	14	acoustic guitar
3	synthesizers	7	microphone	11	dancers	15	bass guitar
4	loudspeakers	8	drummer	12	saxophone player	16	lead guitar

The theatre

1 (page 62)

1 – m 5 – f 9 – d 12 – l
2 – i 6 – a 10 – g 13 – c
3 – b 7 – n 11 – j 14 – e
4 – h 8 – k

2 (pages 63 and 64)

1	box office	5	dress rehearsal	9	stage	14	wings
2	foyer	6	stalls ... circle	10	first night	15	interval
	... auditorium		(or balcony)	11	(orchestra) pit	16	rehearse
3	performance	7	matinée	12	programme	17	dressing-room
4	aisle ... row	8	applause	13	curtain		

The cinema

1 (page 65)

5	action/adventure	12	drama	13	horror film	9	science fiction
	film	1	disaster movie	6	juvenile film		film
14	cartoon	10	fantasy film	2	love story	11	thriller
7	comedy	4	foreign film	15	musical	3	war film
						8	western

2 (pages 66, 67 and 68)

Suggestion

1	Juvenile film	5	Action/adventure	8	Thriller	12	Love story
2	Science fiction		film	9	Musical	13	Fantasy film
	film	6	Western	10	Comedy	14	Cartoon
3	War film	7	Foreign film	11	Drama	15	Horror film
4	Disaster movie						

Other forms of entertainment (page 69)

No right or wrong answers.

Phrasal verbs

1 (page 70)

1	– d	4	– c	7	– j	9	– b
2	– g	5	– f	8	– e	10	– h
3	– i	6	– a				

2 (page 71)

1	given (them) up	4	Work (it) out	7	cut off	9	took up
2	put on	5	break up	8	look after	10	gone off
3	brought (him) up	6	let (me) off				

Check 1

(pages 72 and 73)

1	(d) predecessor	5	(a) an old	8	(a) the hard
2	(c) giddy		people's home		shoulder
3	(b) an accountant	6	(c) punctual	9	(d) Road works
4	(b) your landlord	7	(d) a clutch	10	(b) a barge

11 (page 73) *Suggestions only. Other answers may be possible.*

(a) buffet car *(All the others are to do with travelling by plane.)*

(b) cheerful *(All the others are negative traits.)*

(c) package tour *(All the others are places to stay on holiday.)*

(d) Australian *(All the other are languages.)* or Flemish *(All the others are nationalities.)*

(e) cello *(You blow all the other instruments.)*

12 (page 73)

13 (page 74)

(a) lodger
(b) orphan
(c) forgetful
(d) envious
(e) childminder
(f) yawning
(g) crawl
(h) litter bin
(i) level crossing
(j) overtake

14 (page 74)

a bachelor	is not married
a celebrity	is famous
an employee	works for someone
an heir	will inherit
an invalid	is disabled or ill
an optimist	looks on the bright side of life
a racist	dislikes foreigners
a refugee	has left his or her country
a vegetarian	never eats meat
a widow	no longer has a husband

15 (page 75)

(a) C

(b) I *(A survivor is someone who lives after an accident.)*

(c) C

(d) I *(It should be self-conscious.)*

(e) C

(f) I *(A governor is in charge of a prison. An editor is in charge of a newspaper.)*

(g) I *(You just close one eye. You close two when you blink.)*

(h) C

(i) C

(j) I *(A prompter does that. An usher shows you to your seat.)*

16 (page 75)

The missing words are:
attractive, dark–skinned, early, medium build, above average height, shoulder-length, fringe

17 (page 76)

The lines are in the following order:
5 – 12 – 8 – 11 – 3 – 1 – 9 – 6 – 2 – 10 – 13 – 4 – 7

18 (pages 76 and 77)

(a) turn up	(d) broke down	(g) go with	(i) fill in
(b) look (it) up	(e) called (it) off	(h) break up	(j) gave up
(c) put on	(f) take up		

19 (page 78)

8 aisle	**3** curtain	**5** orchestra pit	**2** stage
12 box office	**1** dressing-room	**9** programme	**6** stalls
10 circle/balcony	**11** foyer	**7** row	**4** wings

20 (page 79)

Musical instruments	At the seaside	In the town
accordion	beach	building site
bongoes	cliff	kerb
harp	deck-chair	lamp-post
synthesizer	pier	pavement
tuba	wave	pillar box

Travelling by road	Travelling by plane	Travelling by train
by-pass	airport	carriage
diversion	baggage reclaim	inter-city express
motorway	boarding pass	platform
outside lane	check-in desk	restaurant car
roundabout	departure lounge	ticket collector

21 (pages 80 and 81)

Across

1 indicator switch **6** glove compartment **9** horn **12** ignition **13** tyre
16 speedometer **19** rear light **21** accelerator **22** clutch **23** boot

Down

2 indicator **3** handbrake **4** bonnet **5** steering wheel **6** gear lever **7** exhaust pipe
8 aerial **10** wing **11** wheel **14** bumper **15** headlight **16** seatbelt **17** dashboard
18 car radio **20** lock

Section Four: Education, books and the media

In the classroom (page 82)

20	biro/ballpoint pen	23	(a pair of) compasses	11	overhead projector	24	ruler
5	(black)board	6	cupboard	25	pencil	2	satchel/ schoolbag
8	bookcase	13	desk	18	pencil sharpener	19	set square
26	calculator	14	duster	27	protractor	7	shelf
16	calendar	4	exercise book	1	pupil	3	textbook
9	(a piece of) chalk	21	felt-tip pen	22	rubber	12	timetable
		15	globe			10	wall chart
		17	glue				

British schools and institutions (pages 83 and 84)

8	boarding school	14	evening classes	2	private school	1	state school
18	co-educational school	4	nursery school	16	public school	11	Teacher Training College
12	College of Further Education	7	playschool	6	secondary school	13	The Open University
		15	Polytechnic				
9	comprehensive school	10	prep school	17	Sixth-Form College	5	university
		3	primary school				

Follow up (page 85)

Schools for children under 5

nursery school
playschool

State schools (5–18)

comprehensive school
primary school
Sixth Form College

Private schools (5–18)

prep school
public school

**Higher education
(people who have left school)**

College of Further Education
Polytechnic
Teacher Training College
university

Who's who in education (pages 86 and 87)

1	– e	5	– b	9	– a	13	– c
2	– n	6	– m	10	– g	14	– k
3	– h	7	– d	11	– i	15	– f
4	– j	8	– l	12	– o		

Verbs to do with education (pages 88 and 89)

1	left school	6	specialize	10	behave	14	sit/take
2	praised	7	enrol	11	failed	15	test
3	revise	8	learn … by heart … recite	12	doing (her) homework	16	play truant
4	attend	9	study	13	punished	17	pass
5	expel						

Other useful words to do with education (pages 90 and 91)

1	form	6	vacation	11	compulsory	15	course
2	mark	7	deputy head	12	detention	16	playground
3	scholarship	8	lecture	13	seminar	17	tutorial
4	subjects	9	assignment	14	academic	18	gymnasium
5	register	10	staff room		... terms		
	... present						
	... absent						

Types of books (pages 92 and 93)

14	anthology	12	cookery book	3	manual	17	romantic novel
6	atlas	2	dictionary	16	memoirs	20	science fiction
8	autobiography	9	directory	7	non-fiction		novel
18	best seller	1	encyclopedia	11	paperback	10	textbook
23	biography	4	fiction	22	poetry book	13	thriller
19	book of fairy	15	guidebook	24	reference book	5	whodunnit
	tales	21	hardback				

Follow up (pages 94 and 95)

1	book of fairy	4	guidebook	7	science fiction	9	poetry book
	tales	5	cookery book		novel	10	whodunnit
2	manual	6	romantic novel	8	autobiography	11	thriller
3	biography					12	dictionary

Parts of a book (pages 96 and 97)

1	cover	5	illustrations	8	chapter	12	contents
2	jacket	6	acknowledge-	9	appendix	13	glossary
3	title		ments	10	foreword	14	footnote
4	bibliography	7	preface	11	index	15	blurb

The media: Television

Types of programme (pages 98 and 99)

The missing programme types are:

1	– d	5	– b	12	– a	14	– h
3	– f	6	– i	13	– e	16	– c
4	– j	10	– g				

Follow up (page 100)

1	educational	4	music	7	news and	9	food
	programme		programme		current affairs		programme
2	nature	5	detective series		programme	10	drama series
	programme	6	travel	8	quiz show		
3	documentary		programme				

The media: Newspapers

Useful words to do with newspapers (pages 101, 102 and 103)

1	headline	9	weather forecast	15	colour	21	review
2	editor	10	quality papers		supplement	22	journalist
3	circulation		... popular	16	obituary		... reporter
4	letters page		papers	17	correspondent	23	feature
5	sports pages	11	caption	18	editorial	24	crossword
6	article	12	comic strip	19	classified		
7	advertisements	13	column		advertisements		
8	horoscope	14	gossip column	20	tabloid		

Follow up (pages 103 and 104)

1	weather	4	review	7	classified	10	comic strip
	forecast	5	letters page		advertisements	11	caption
2	headline	6	obituary	8	horoscope	12	crossword
3	gossip column			9	sports page		

A newspaper article (page 105)

The lines are in the following order:

5 – 10 – 15 – 1 – 18 – 11 – 14 – 7 – 4 – 2 – 9 – 12 – 17 – 3 – 13 – 8 – 16 – 6

Phrasal verbs

1 (page 106)

1	– d	4	– j	7	– e	9	– g
2	– h	5	– a	8	– b	10	– c
3	– f	6	– i				

2 (page 107)

1	got over	4	take off	7	came round	9	fell out
2	look up to	5	look at	8	takes after	10	look for
3	came across	6	picked (it) up				

Section Five: Word-building

Prefixes 1 (pages 108 and 109)

1	dishonest	4	informal	7	misprint	9	disagree
2	irresponsible	5	rewrite	8	independent	10	dislike
3	disadvantage	6	incorrect				

Prefixes 2 (page 109)

1	impatient	4	uncertain	7	untrue	9	impolite
2	unfriendly	5	non-violence	8	uncomfortable	10	unemployed
3	illegal	6	impossible				

Follow up (pages 110 and 111)

dis-	il-	im-	in-
appear	literate	mature	complete
loyal	logical	moral	consistent
obey			expensive
satisfied			experienced
			human

ir-	mis-	non-	un-
regular	behave	fiction	common
relevant	treat	smoker	expected
	understand		fortunately
			happy
			lucky

Suffixes: Changing words into nouns for people (page 112)

1	librarian	4	artist	7	politician	10	collector
2	survivor	5	director	8	guitarist	11	electrician
3	owner	6	writer	9	terrorist	12	manager

Suffixes: Changing words into adjectives 1 (page 113)

1	frightening	4	homeless	7	useless	10	painless
2	windy	5	angry	8	doubtful	11	exciting
3	careful	6	healthy	9	boring	12	beautiful

Suffixes: Changing words into adjectives 2 (page 114)

1	dangerous	4	creative	7	comfortable	10	musical
2	optimistic	5	reliable	8	famous	11	courageous
3	central	6	accidental	9	artistic	12	attractive

Suffixes: Changing words into nouns 1 (page 115)

1	difficulty	4	apology	7	arrival	10	performance
2	intelligence	5	importance	8	discovery	11	difference
3	trial	6	refusal	9	absence	12	Insurance

Suffixes: Changing words into nouns 2 (page 116)

1	election	4	mileage	7	marriage	10	invitation
2	pronunciation	5	suggestion	8	discussion	11	description
3	invention	6	Education	9	explosion	12	postage

Suffixes: Changing words into nouns 3 (page 117)

1	disappointment	4	weakness	7	activity	10	darkness
2	sadness	5	equality	8	treatment	11	popularity
3	advertisement	6	arrangement	9	government	12	illness

Changing words into nouns 4 (various endings) (page 118)

1	knowledge	4	loss	7	heat	10	death
2	signature	5	strength	8	height	11	length
3	depth	6	choice	9	anger	12	flight

Changing nouns into adjectives (various endings) (pages 119 and 120)

1	ambitious	6	legal/illegal	11	national	16	southern
2	cloudy	7	lucky	12	poisonous	17	successful
3	daily	8	medical	13	professional	18	sympathetic
4	helpful	9	mountainous	14	reasonable	19	tasteless
5	hungry	10	mysterious	15	sensible	20	useful

Changing adjectives into nouns (various endings) (pages120 and 1221)

1	ability	6	envy	11	happiness	16	reality
2	beauty	7	fame	12	health	17	shortage
3	boredom	8	freedom	13	horror	18	thirst
4	distance	9	friendship	14	poverty	19	truth
5	ease	10	gratitude	15	pride	20	value

Changing verbs into nouns (various endings) (pages 122 and 123)

1	appearance	6	decision	11	meeting	16	robbery
2	behaviour	7	departure	12	painting	17	service
3	belief	8	destruction	13	permission	18	speech
4	comparison	9	entertainment	14	pleasure	19	translation
5	competition	10	information	15	proof	20	weight

Nouns from phrasal verbs

1 (page 124)

1	– f	4	– h	7	– d	9	– g
2	– j	5	– a	8	– b	10	– c
3	– e	6	– i				

2 (pages 125 and 126)

1	downpour	4	write-up	7	output	9	break-in
2	write-off	5	drawback	8	check-up	10	hold-up
3	breakdown	6	break-up				

Section Six: Adjectives, verbs and prepositions

Adjectives: Synonyms (page 127)

1	terrible	6	glad	11	silent	16	famous
2	expensive	7	eager	12	impolite	17	evil
3	boring	8	crazy	13	unhappy	18	broad
4	scared	9	well-mannered	14	peculiar	19	marvellous
5	attractive	10	fast	15	enormous	20	incorrect

Adjectives: Opposites (pages 128 and 129)

1	loose	5	absent	9	mean	13	alive
2	shallow	6	noisy	10	public	14	exciting
3	tame	7	single	11	asleep	15	odd
4	imaginary	8	amateur	12	stale	16	lazy

Useful adjectives 1 (pages 129 and 130)

1	guilty	5	busy	9	healthy	13	dangerous
2	popular	6	noisy	10	chilly	14	favourite
3	valuable	7	secret	11	serious	15	rusty
4	different	8	delicious	12	juicy	16	fashionable

Useful adjectives 2 (pages 130 and 131)

1	necessary	5	natural	9	regular	13	deaf
2	slippery	6	rotten	10	disappointing	14	ripe
3	willing	7	blind	11	risky	15	excellent
4	average	8	useful	12	temporary	16	practical

Verbs: Synonyms (page 132)

1	permit	6	weep	11	occur	16	repair
2	inquire	7	vanish	12	detest	17	require
3	brag	8	stumble	13	assist	18	bathe
4	purchase	9	scare	14	depart	19	speak
5	alter	10	enter	15	adore	20	attempt

Verbs: Opposites (pages 133 and 134)

1	destroy	5	won	9	vanished	13	catch
2	succeeded	6	contracts	10	arrive	14	rejected
3	can't stand	7	admit	11	save	15	demolish
4	mend	8	lowering	12	defend	16	allow

Useful verbs 1 (page 135)

1	– i	5	– g	9	– o	13	– l
2	– d	6	– n	10	– b	14	– c
3	– m	7	– k	11	– p	15	– j
4	– a	8	– e	12	– f	16	– h

Useful verbs 2 (page 136)

1	– e	5	– a	9	– n	13	– j
2	– k	6	– o	10	– l	14	– f
3	– g	7	– i	11	– p	15	– h
4	– m	8	– d	12	– b	16	– c

Useful verbs 3 (pages 137 and 138)

1	lock	6	repeat	11	worry	16	visit
2	was shining	7	understand	12	apologized	17	arrange
3	waste	8	afford	13	hurts	18	obey
4	decide	9	ends	14	smile	19	cause
5	fix	10	screamed	15	fit	20	refused

174

Useful verbs 4 (pages 138 and 139)

1	demanded	6	trust	11	hid	16	avoid
2	multiply	7	admired	12	contains	17	pretended
3	Remind	8	follows	13	produce	18	blame
4	belongs to	9	rush	14	continue	19	behave
5	fetch	10	annoys	15	doubt	20	point

Verbs that usually follow certain nouns (page 140)

1	– i	5	– d	9	– g	13	– o
2	– m	6	– n	10	– e	14	– k
3	– f	7	– a	11	– p	15	– c
4	– l	8	– j	12	– b	16	– h

Verbs to do with movement (pages 141 and 142)

1	hop	5	bent down	9	staggered	13	sliding
2	strolled	6	throw	10	cycle	14	marched
3	chased	7	climb	11	stand	15	limping
4	ride	8	jump	12	dashed	16	Pick (them) up

Verbs to do with speaking and looking (pages 142 and 143)

1	noticing	6	yelled	10	catch (the	13	swore
2	stuttered	7	stared		waiter's) eye	14	confessed
3	gazed	8	gossips	11	peeped	15	glanced
4	grumbled	9	whispered	12	examined	16	peered
5	announced						

Prepositions with nouns (pages 143 and 144)

1	by	4	at	7	For	9	on
2	in	5	by	8	in	10	FOR
3	on	6	at				

Prepositions with adjectives (pages 144 and 145)

1	to	6	to	11	at	16	to
2	in	7	for	12	with	17	of
3	with	8	of	13	of	18	for
4	at	9	with	14	for	19	to
5	of	10	in	15	with	20	for

Prepositions with verbs (pages 146 and 147)

1	from	6	in	11	on	16	to
2	of	7	to	12	about	17	at
3	with	8	of	13	from	18	in
4	for	9	for	14	on	19	OF
5	at	10	with	15	for	20	about

Three-part phrasal verbs

1 (page 148)

1	– f	4	– g	7	– b	9	– h
2	– i	5	– a	8	– j	10	– d
3	– e	6	– c				

2 (page 149)

1 face up to
2 hang on to
3 make up for
4 drop in on
5 stand in for
6 look back on
7 drop out of
8 get along/on with
9 get around/ round to
10 look out for

Check 2

(pages 150 and 151)

1 (b) wall chart
2 (a) played truant
3 (d) a protractor
4 (b) a prep school
5 (d) an undergraduate
6 (b) a register
7 (a) the jacket
8 (d) a thriller
9 (c) a chat show
10 (c) the gossip column

11 (page 151) *Suggestions only. Other answers may be possible.*

(a) calculator *(All the others are classroom fixtures or furniture.)*

(b) secondary school *(All the others offer education/training after you leave school.)*

(c) caretaker *(All the others are in charge of schools, colleges, etc.)*

(d) whodunnit *(All the other are non-fiction.)*

(e) chapter *(All the other words are to do with a newspaper.)*

12 (page 152)

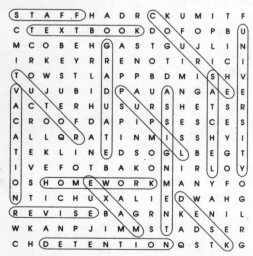

13 (pages 152 and 153)

(a) duster
(b) enrol
(c) deputy head
(d) best seller
(e) chapters
(f) circulation
(g) obituary
(h) dishonest
(i) comfortable
(j) unemployed

14 (page 153)

attend	a course	punish her	for not doing her homework
behave	badly at the party		
learn a poem	by heart	recite	a poem
leave school	at the age of 17	study	for an exam
pass	a driving test	specialize	in foreign languages
praise her	for her excellent work		

15 (pages 153 and 154)

(a) I *(That would be a telescope or pair of binoculars. An overhead projector shows overhead transparencies.)*
(b) C
(c) C
(d) I *(It is about imaginary characters and events.)*
(e) C
(f) C *(The opposite is voluntary)*
(g) I *(It is much smaller.)*
(h) C *(It means regain consciousness after fainting.)*
(i) I *(It should be break-in.)*
(j) I *(She's blind. You can't hear when you are deaf.)*

16 (pages 154 and 155)

(a) arrival
(b) insurance
(c) description
(d) invention
(e) disappointment
(f) weakness
(g) depth
(h) knowledge
(i) boredom
(j) poverty
(k) fame
(l) appearance
(m) competition
(n) permission
(o) speech

17 (page 155)

(a) boring
(b) broad
(c) dear
(d) enormous
(e) peculiar
(f) weep
(g) vanish
(h) attempt
(i) enter
(j) scare

18 (page 156)

(a) absent
(b) lazy
(c) imaginary
(d) shallow
(e) stale
(f) admit
(g) accept
(h) defend
(i) destroy
(j) save

19 (page 156)

(a) on
(b) on
(c) with
(d) of
(e) at
(f) in
(g) from
(h) of
(i) with
(j) from

20 (pages 156 and 157)

(a) takes after
(b) picked (it) up
(c) fallen out
(d) breakdown
(e) downpour
(f) drop in on
(g) get along/on with
(h) hang on to
(i) standing in for
(j) looking back on

21 (page 158)

Things you write with	People in education	Other words to do with education
ballpoint pen	expert	academic
biro	governor	lecture
chalk	graduate	seminar
felt-tip pen	student	term
pencil	tutor	tutorial

Types of books	Parts of a book	Parts of a newspaper
anthology	acknowledgements	article
autobiography	bibliography	classified ads
encyclopedia	blurb	headline
memoirs	contents	review
romantic novel	index	sports page

Key words

The number after each word refers to the section in which the word appears

ability 5
able 5
above average height 1
absence 5
absent 4, 5, 6
academic 4
accelerate 2
accelerator 2
accident 5
accidental 5
accordion 3
accountant 1
acknowledgements 4
acoustic guitar 3
acquaintance 1
action film 3
active 5
activity 5
actor 3
actress 3
addicted to 6
admire 6
admit 6
adore 6
advantage 5
adventure story 3
advertise 5
advertise for 6
advertisement 2, 5
advertisements 4
aerial 2
affectionate 1
afford 6
afraid 1
agree 5
airline ticket 2
airport 2
aisle 2, 3
alive 6
allergic to 6
allow 6
alter 6
amateur 6
ambition 5

ambitious 5
ambulance 2
amplifier 3
ancestor 1
anger 5
angry 1, 5
angry with (someone) 6
announce 6
annoy 6
anthology 4
apologize 5, 6
apologize for 6
apology 5
appear 5
appearance 5
appendix 4
applause 3
apply for 6
apprentice 4
arrange 5, 6
arrangement 5
arrival 5
arrive 5, 6
arrogant 1
art 5
article 4
artist 5
artistic 5
ashamed 1
ashamed of 6
Asia 3
ask 6
asleep 6
assignment 4
assist 6
at (first) 6
at (the moment) 6
atlas 4
attempt 6
attend 4
attract 5
attractive 1, 5, 6
audience 3
auditorium 3

Australian 3
Austrian 3
autobiography 4
average 6
avoid 6
awful 6

bachelor 1
backing group 3
bad-tempered 1
baggage reclaim 2
bagpipes 3
baker 1
balcony 3
ballpoint pen 4
banjo 3
bank holiday 3
barge 2
barrister 1
bass guitar 3
bassoon 3
bathe 6
bays 3
be called 6
beach 3
beach hut 3
beach-ball 3
beaches 3
beat 6
beautiful 5
beauty 5
beauty spot 3
bed and breakfast 3
behave 4, 5, 6
behaviour 5
Belgian 3
belief 5
believe 5
believe in 6
belong to 6
below average height 1
bend down 6
Bend to right (road sign) 2

179

organ 3
orphan 1
output 5
outside lane 2
overhead projector 4
overtake 2
owe 6
own (verb) 5
owner 5

package tour 3
pain 5
painless 5
paint 5
painting 5
palm trees 3
paperback 4
park (verb) 2
parking meter 2
partner 1
pass (verb) 4
passenger seat 2
passport 2
passport control 2
patient (adjective) 1, 5
pavement 2
peculiar 6
pedestrian 1
pedestrian crossing 2
pedestrian precinct 2
peep 6
peer 6
pencil 4
pencil sharpener 4
perform 5
performance 3, 5
permission 5
permit (verb) 5, 6
pessimist 1
pessimistic 1
petrol cap 2
petrol gauge 2
photographer 1
phrase-book 3
piano 3
pick up (*a language*) 4
pick up (*something on ground*) 6
pick-up truck 2
picturesque 3
pier 3
pillar box 2
plane 2
platform 2
play (noun) 4

playing bingo 3
playing bridge 3
playing golf 3
playing pool 3
playing squash 3
play truant 4
playground 4
playschool 4
playwright 3
please (verb) 5
pleasure 5
plumber 1
plump 1
poetry book 4
point 6
poison 5
poisonous 5
police car 2
Polish 3
polite 5, 6
politician 5
politics 5
Polytechnic 4
poor 5
popular 5, 6
popular papers 4
popular with 6
popularity 5
Portuguese 3
possible 5
post (verb) 5
postage 5
postman 1
postpone 6
poverty 5
practical 6
practise 6
practise speaking a foreign language 3
praise (verb) 4
predecessor 1
preface 4
prefer to 6
prep school 4
present (adjective) 4
president 1
pretend 6
pretty 1
pride 5
primary school 4
prime minister 1
principal 1, 4
print 5
private school 4
produce 6

profession 5
professional 5
programme 3
prompter 3
pronounce 5, 6
pronunciation 5
proof 5
protractor 4
proud 1, 5
prove 5
psychiatrist 1
public 6
public conveniences 2
public school 4
punctual 1
punish 4, 6
pupil 4
purchase 6
put off 1
put on 3
put through 2
put up with 2

quality papers 4
quarrel with 6
quick 6
quiet 6
quite old 1
quite tall 1
quite young 1
quiz show 4

racist 1
railway station 2
real 5
reality 5
rear light 2
rear window 2
rear-view mirror 2
reason 5
reasonable 5
receptionist 1
recite 4
reference book 4
refugee 1
refusal 5
refuse 5, 6
register (noun) 4
regular 5, 6
rehearse 3
reject 6
relevant 5
reliable 1, 5
relieved 1
rely 5

remind 6
remind of 6
renew 6
repair 6
repeat 6
reporter 4
require 6
resort 3
responsible 5
responsible for 6
restaurant car 2
restaurants 3
restless 1
return (*ticket*) 2
return (verb) 6
reverse 2
review 4
revise 4
rewrite 5
ride (verb) 6
ring (*a doorbell*) 6
ripe 6
rise (*the sun*) 6
risky 6
rival 1
Road narrows (*road sign*) 2
road sign 2
Road works (*road sign*) 2
rob 5
robbery 5
romantic novel 4
roof rack 2
rotten 6
roundabout 2
row (noun) 3
rowing boat 2
rubber 4
rude 6
ruler 4
rush 6
Russian 3
rusty 6

sad 5, 6
sadness 5
saloon car 2
sand 3
sandcastle 3
satchel 4
satisfied 5
save 6
saxophone 3
saxophone player 3
scare 6

scared 6
scenery 3
scholar 4
scholarship 4
School crossing patrol (*road sign*) 2
schoolbag 4
science fiction film 3
science fiction novel 4
scientist 1
scooter 2
scream (verb) 6
scuba diving 3
sea 3
sea wall 3
seat-belt 2
secondary school 4
secret (adjective) 6
secretary 1
security check 2
self-catering 3
self-confident 1
self-conscious 1
selfish 1
seminar 4
send postcards home 3
sense 5
sensible 5
sensitive 1
serious 6
serve 5
service 5
service area 2
set designer 3
set off 2
set square 4
shallow 6
shelf 4
shine 6
shiver 6
shocked 1
shop assistant 1
short 5
shortage 5
shoulder length 1
sightseeing 3
sign (verb) 5
signature 5
silent 6
single 6
sit/take (*an exam*) 4
Sixth-Form College 4
skid 2
skinny 1
sleepy 1

slide 6
slip road 2
slippery 6
smell (verb) 1
smile (verb) 1, 6
smoker 5
sneeze 1
soap opera 4
social worker 1
solve 6
sorry for 6
south 5
southern 5
spa 3
spade 3
Spanish 3
speak 5, 6
specialize 4
spectacular 3
spectator 1
speech 5
speedboat 2
speedometer 2
spend 6
spinster 1
sports car 2
sports page 4
sports programme 4
spy film 3
staff 4
staff-room 4
stage 3
stage hand 3
stage manager 3
stagger 6
stale 6
stall (verb) 2
stalls 3
stand (verb) 6
stand in for 6
stare 6
Start of motorway (*road sign*) 2
state school 4
steering wheel 2
stockbroker 1
straight 1
strange 6
strength 5
strict 1
stroll 6
strong 5
stubborn 1
student 4
study 4

stumble 6
stutter 6
subjects 4
subway 2
succeed 6
success 5
successful 5
successful in 6
successor 1
suggest 5
suggestion 5
suitable for 6
sunbathing 3
sunshine 3
sure of 6
surprised at 6
survive 5
survivor 1, 5
swear 6
swept back 1
swim 6
swim in the pool 3
swimmer 3
Swiss 3
sympathetic 1, 5
sympathy 5
synthesizer 3

tabloid 4
take after 4
take lots of photographs 3
take off (*leave ground*) 1
take off (*clothing*) 4
take up 3
talk 6
talkative 1
tambourine 3
tame 6
tanned 1
taste (noun) 5
taste (verb) 6
tasteless 5
taxi 2
taxi rank 2
teacher 1
Teacher Training College 4
telephone box 2
temporary 6
tenant 1
tense (adjective) 1
Terminal 2
terms 4
terrible 6
terror 5

terrorist 5
test 4
textbook 4
The Open University 4
thirst 5
thirsty 5
thriller 3, 4
through train 2
throw 6
throw at 6
ticket collector 2
ticket office 2
tickets 2
timetable 2, 4
title 4
took off 2
touch 1
tourist 1
tower block 2
traffic island 2
traffic lights 2
traffic warden 1
train 2
tram 2
translate 5, 6
translate from 6
translation 5
travel programme 4
treat 5
treatment 5
trial 5
triangle 3
trip 3
trolley 2
trombone 3
true 5
trumpet 3
trust 6
truth 5
try 5, 6
tuba 3
Turkish 3
turn down 2
turn up 1
tutor 4
tutorial 4
TV film 4
twin 1
tyre 2

umpire 1
uncertain 5
uncomfortable 5
uncommon 5
undergraduate 4

underpass 2
understand 5, 6
understudy 3
undertaker 1
unemployed 5
Uneven road (*road sign*) 2
unexpected 5
unfortunately 5
unfriendly 5
unhappy 5, 6
university 4
unlucky 5
unpack 6
unspoilt 3
untrue 5
upset 1
use 5
useful 5, 6
useless 5
usher 3
usherette 3

vacation 4
vain 1
valuable 5, 6
value 5
van 2
vanish 6
vegetarian 1
very big 6
vice-chancellor 4
victim 1
view 3
viola 3
violence 5
violin 3
visa 3
visit 6
visit museums and art
    galleries 3

wall chart 4
war film 3
warden 1
wash up 6
waste 6
watching football 3
watching television 3
wave (noun) 3
wave (verb) 6
weak 5
weakness 5
weather forecast 4
wedding anniversary 3
weep 6

weigh 5, 6
weight 5
well-behaved 1
well-known 6
well-mannered 6
Welsh 3
western 3
wheel 2
whisper 6
whistle 1
whodunnit 4
wicked 6
wide 6
widow 1
willing 6

win (verb) 6
wind 5
window seat 2
windscreen 2
windscreen wiper 2
windy 5
wing 2
wing mirror 2
wings 3
wink (verb) 1
with a fringe 1
with a parting 1
witty 1
wonderful 6

work out 3
worry 6
worry about 6
write 5
write to 6
write-off 5
write-up 5
writer 5
wrong 6

yacht 2
yawn 1
yell 6
youth hostel 3